'Missy Baba'
to
'Burra Mem'

Joan and Geoffrey Allen back home in 1971
(note skin of marauding leopard at their feet)

'Missy Baba'
to
'Burra Mem'

The life of a Planter's daughter in northern India, 1913-1970

by

Joan Allen

BACSA

PUTNEY, LONDON
1998

Published by the British Association
for Cemeteries in South Asia (BACSA)

Secretary: Theon Wilkinson MBE
76½ Chartfield Avenue
London SW15 6HQ

The British Association for Cemeteries in South Asia was formed in 1976 to
preserve, convert and record old European cemeteries.
All proceeds from the sale of this book go towards this charity
(Registered No 273422)

ISBN 0 907799 60 4

British Libraries Cataloguing-in-Publication Data
A catalogue record for this book is available from the British Library

Cover designed and map adapted by Rosemarie Wilkinson

Typeset by Professional Presentation, 3 Prairie Road, Addlestone, Surrey

Printed by The Chameleon Press Ltd., 5-25 Burr Road, Wandsworth SW18 4SG

Contents

Illustrations

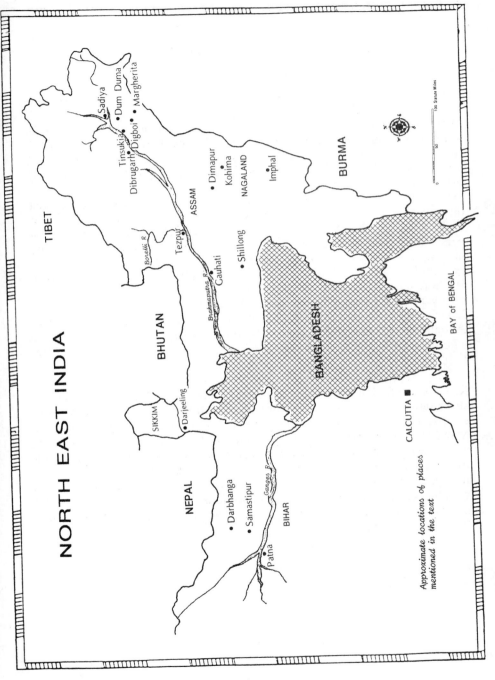

NORTH EAST INDIA

Approximate locations of places
mentioned in the text

Foreword

Missy Baba to Burra Mem - The Life of a Planter's Daughter in Northern India 1913-1970 is the twenty-eighth in a series of books about Europeans in South Asia, written by BACSA members (in this case the mother of two BACSA members), published by BACSA for its members with a wider public in mind.

'Missy Baba' was the affectionate title given to young English girls in India, often by the servants, but 'Burra Mem' was something very grand that the senior memsahibs only became after many years there. The book is an evocative personal account of a girl growing up in a Planter's environment in Bihar, meeting and marrying a Planter, Geoffrey Allen, who then goes off to the War as a Gurkha Officer, while she is left with their children, with no fixed home, awaiting news. Eventually she learns that he has been captured at Tobruk, is a prisoner of war in Italy, has escaped and returns to take part in the War against Japan on the north-east frontier. Meanwhile she becomes involved in war-work in Shillong and later, after the end of hostilities, in supporting his new career as a Political Officer in the north-east tribal areas of Assam, and finally in the Tea Industry.

Readers will find in the book descriptions of incidents in family life which will strike familiar chords of memory interlaced with fascinating details of unusual experiences - the great Bihar earthquake of 1934, elephant processions with the Maharaja of Darbhanga, life on a plantation with its long periods of loneliness, mixed with short 'Meets' of exhilarating entertainments, and life among the tribals in one of the remotest corners of the world, where news of India's Independence hardly penetrated. The author is a member of the Allen family with roots in Cawnpore, publishing connections with Kipling and involvement in India extending to the present day through the careers of her children. She now lives quietly in the New Forest.

Acknowledgements

With thanks for their help
to Marie Andrews and the rest
of the Ringwood Writers Circle

In loving memory
to two very dear men,
my husband and my father

1
Beginnings in Bihar
1896-1913

The world has now become small and familiar, toddlers have probably heard of places in Africa, Australia, or China, even spent holidays in Spain, or Greece. Nowhere is entirely strange with television bringing foreign countries into the sitting room.

It was not like that in 1896, when my father, John Henry, aged twenty-one, sailed from his home in Ulster to work in India. Rules on board ship were rigid, correct dress to meals was a must, with coat and tie always worn, with dinner jackets and stiff shirts for the evening.

A bugle would sound before the first course was served, and another before the next, and so on. If you were late you missed that course, so that you missed whatever courses had been served. The heavy drinkers had to choose between that extra tot of gin or some pudding.

My father did not leave India again until he volunteered to fight in the Boer War, during the early 1900s. Young indigo planters from Bihar like him, men from the jute industry in Bengal, and officewallahs from Calcutta were all keen to join up.

A subscription was made to form a Troop called Lumsden's Horse, under the command of Colonel Lumsden, a Calcutta man. This unit, in which my father was only a humble trooper, did sterling duty in Africa during the Boer War, after which it was disbanded.

All who had survived united to pay for a memorial in the shape of a silver cup on a wooden plinth. On the cup itself were engraved the names of all who lost their lives in the fighting. Inside the hollow stand was placed a list bearing the names of all who had served in the unique unit, my father's among them.

The strange aftermath was that when in the 1970s my eldest son, Michael, was Brigade Major of the Brigade of Gurkhas, serving in Hong Kong, there was a dinner in the Mess of the Brigade of Gurkhas to which General Chapple was invited.

The Boer War came up in the conversation, and Michael mentioned that his grandfather had served in it in a Volunteer Force from India called Lumsden's Horse. 'Well,' said the General, 'we can prove if that is correct because here, in the Mess, we have the Lumsden's Horse Memorial Cup.'

The Mess Sergeant collected the cup and a screwdriver. The General opened up the plinth and there was the record of the survivors, with the name of John Henry, Michael's grandfather, among them. Michael has told me how relieved he was to see it there.

This may have been the first time in nearly seventy years this list had been seen, and it gave my son a great thrill, as well as relief. A toast was drunk to the memory of Lumsden's Horse. There is another link in this chain but I will refer to this much later.

After this martial interlude, my father returned to his work in Bihar as an assistant to an indigo planter. When he had first arrived as a newly joined assistant, he was immediately called a Creeper, the term for the lowliest of the low. When the two Merrick brothers arrived together, the eldest was automatically a Creeper, but how to distinguish his younger brother? He became known as a Crawler. The names stuck to this pair. Many years later when I came to know them, in their middle age they were still Creeper and Crawler, in spite of the fact that indigo planting which had given them their names was a thing of the past. Why it was ever Creeper, I cannot imagine, because nothing that I know about indigo seems to warrant it. It began to replace woad in about the 16th century, but was never manufactured on a big scale until the 19th, so when my father became an indigo planter in 1896, it was in full production, Bihar being a major producer of good quality dye. Indigo is a bush, the *Indigoferra Tinctorio*, which grew to about five feet; when it flowered the buds were discarded, the plant cut to the ground and collected into bundles for steeping in vats of water. The roots sprout again, but the yield of colour grows progressively less; five years is the outside limit for a plant.

When steeped, fermentation produced a straw-coloured liquid, which was drained off into other vats; there the liquid was stirred, and agitated by the labourer standing waist high in it. This caused the colour to change, and various alkali, such as lime, were added, the result strained, and boiled until hard, gritty cakes were formed which was the indigo dye. No heavy machinery was needed in the process.

Life for the young assistants on indigo plantations, the Creepers, was a lonely one; there was little entertainment for them or their managers, or their wives if they had them, living in isolated bungalows. There was one occasion to which all looked forward throughout the year. This was the Meet. Over the length and breadth of Bihar, each District HQ had its Meet, a week a year given over to fun and games.

For my father his HQ was Muzaffarpur and the residents of the town from the Judge, and the District Commissioner, down to the most junior engineer in the Public Works Department threw open their bungalows, put up tents in their gardens, stocked up with supplies, and made ready for the invasion. To be exact they told their servants to get everything prepared as usual.

For miles around in North Bihar everyone who could headed for the town, British government servants, and Police officers from the Sub-Divisions, planters of all ages, from those who owned their own estates to the humblest Creeper, all flocked in. Wives were brought, but especially popular were those with nubile daughters or who had unmarried sisters visiting them; girls were in short supply in that society. They came by pony trap, or rode, cars not having reached those parts then. Those near stations came by train, being met by rickshaws, luggage for the rest coming by bullock cart in the care of their bearers, without whom no sahib, or memsahib would go visiting.

The week was spent enjoying themselves, and socialising. Polo was the most important event, but tennis and golf were popular. Gymkhanas (a partially Indian word as *khana* means place) would be held mostly for mounted events. In the evening there was dancing to a small band imported from Calcutta, probably formed of Goan musicians; this was a great treat.

Some years after my father's return from Africa, and when he had become manager of Pandaul, one of the many estates of the Maharaja of Darbhanga, he went to that year's Meet at Muzaffarpur as usual. This one became to him like no other for he met my mother there, and they fell in love at first sight. She was there only for a visit, accompanied by her mother and two sisters, staying with her Uncle Ted on his indigo estate nearby. As you can imagine, he was a popular fellow with three nieces staying with him; he was happy to entertain and have parties, being a cheerful soul. I have been told he had one glass eye, and when he laughed too heartily, it fell out, but he was adept at catching and replacing it. As I have explained these Meets only lasted a week, at the end of which my father, and the other men, had to return to work.

He felt desperate, he had to leave his lovely Mabel not knowing how he could see her again. Her family were only on a short visit. Mrs Exshaw and her daughters would be departing for England, he might never see them again. He could not let this happen. He did return to his work on Pandaul, but each afternoon he rode to the nearest railway station and caught the train to Muzaffarpur. There he got a *tikka gharri*, a rather primitive one horse cab that took him out to Uncle Ted's estate, where he arrived in time for dinner, for Uncle Ted liked entertaining. He spent the evening courting his love, until the *tikka gharri* returned him to the train, which took him to his own station. There he mounted his horse and was back at 6am, the time when planters rode round the fields. All his changing of clothes, washing, shaving and sleeping were done in the train. He continued to do this until my grandmother gave permission for her daughter to marry this persistent young man.

My mother's sisters, Eva and Maggie, had become engaged to Army officers whom they considered to be vastly superior to a mere planter, and not even one with his own estate like their Uncle Ted. They pointed out the dull life she would lead, while they would live in Army cantonments, enjoying plenty of social life. They were right about that, all the social life she had when she married my father were occasional visits by pony and trap to and from neighbours living at least ten miles distant. However, I never heard that she ever complained of her choice. She did have the annual meets, and the bi-annual camps of the Bihar

3

Father and mother on honeymoon, accompanied by Mrs Edna Clarke
who became Joan's godmother

4

Light Horse, a Territorial unit to which most British men belonged. There were Hot and Cold Weather Camps, when the men were all under canvas; while the ladies congregated in convenient bungalows, a chance for a bit of gossip if not much else.

No one in what was called the Mofussil, similar I suppose to the Australian 'outback' had electricity or water laid on then. They had oil lamps, no electric fans, only the hanging *punkah*, pulled by *punkahwallahs*, men who tended to fall asleep; especially at night when an angry and sweaty sahib woke them by heaving a boot through the bedroom door.

Every bedroom did have its own bathroom but do not think of the modern 'en suite' variety. These were rooms divided in two by a low wall, one part with a hole in the outer wall. There the oval tin tub was put, hot water poured into it by the *paniwallah*, the water man, from old kerosene tins, in which he had heated the water probably over an open fire in the back premises. On the low wall stood earthenware jars, called *gylas* in Bihar, which held cold water. The bather could then adjust the bathwater to suit. After the bath was over, and the bather gone, the *paniwallah* would tip up the tub, and the water ran out of the hole in the wall into the drain surrounding the bungalow.

For the most private needs, there was what was generally called the thunderbox, emptied by the sweeper, a man so low in the Hindu caste system he could perform this menial task. It was always wise to look into the pan of the thunderbox before sitting on it, it sometimes harboured strange beasts, especially if it was in a spare room not recently used. Snakes were most feared, but I did hear that someone had found a chicken sitting on her eggs.

Another furnishing of those days was a man's essential, a three legged stool of a convenient height to carry a pot. A story I heard was of a gentleman so short that this convenience was not one to him. When staying with friends, he took to taking his own stool with him. To enable the *paniwallah* and the sweeper to carry out their duties, all bathrooms had two doors, one from the bedroom and the other leading outside.

Very many years later when I had left school and gone out to India to join my father, by then a widower, he was careful to inform me that whenever I went to stay in other people's bungalows always to be sure to keep shut that back door at night. This was not for fear of thieves, or suchlike, but because the back door of a bathroom left open at night was a signal that female company was needed. The servants then arranged for this need to be fulfilled. So at eighteen, and very innocent, I did learn one basic fact of life.

Servants, and mostly such trustworthy ones were something that all sahibs and their mems had in plenty, so at least my mother had no housework to do, not even the usual sewing. Every household had its *darzi*, the tailor, sitting cross-legged on a mat on the back veranda, making and mending for all. Even in my day, we had a cook, a *masalchi*, who washed up, the *paniwallah* for

5

collecting and heating the water, the *khansamah* or *khitmagar* (a butler), two or three bearers (housemen), the sweeper, the *malis* (gardeners), and the *syces* (the grooms). When motor cars came on the scene, drivers were, of course, added to the retinue.

My mother needed a hobby and took up breeding silk worms as hers. Alas, I was too young to get to know about this, but I do know she was a very gifted crocheter. I did not appear for three years after they married, until the end of 1913. There was no hospital available only the *dai*, the village midwife, in whom my father had no confidence. Instead he arranged for a trained monthly nurse to come from Calcutta, a full twenty-four hour rail journey away.

She duly arrived in good time, but I did not. In fact, the whole month for which she was booked passed without my appearance. The nurse got very agitated, but not only on my mother's behalf but mainly because she was due on another case elsewhere in India. My father would not let her leave in spite of her agitation, so she had to stay until I arrived, unscathed in my own good time. I do hope the other mother and baby did not suffer because of me.

2
Life at Darbhanga
(Indigo & Sugar)

As manager of one of the Maharaja's many estates my father was in charge of the indigo production, as well as the cultivation of the plant itself, also that of many other crops grown locally. Much of the land was leased out to tenant farmers in small plots, from whom rents needed collection. All this meant many hours in the saddle, in addition to office and factory work. There were no tractors, or other farm machinery then, all the cultivation was done with bullocks drawing ploughs, a pair yoked together. Bullock carts were the only transport, collecting the harvest, and everything else needed, the well-being of the cattle was important. As was that of the elephants kept as well; they were used for the collection of fodder, but principally were for ceremonial purposes.

On festival occasions, or other important events all the elephants on Pandaul, and the other estates would be rounded up and walked into Darbhanga, twenty miles away, where the Maharaja dwelt in his palaces. There would be processions all round the town led by the Maharaja in his glittering, silver elephant four-in-hand carriage, a vehicle needing a stepladder to mount. Various dignitaries would be honoured by invitations to accompany him. The four elephants drawing it were harnessed two by two, gorgeously caparisoned in velvet robes embroidered with silver thread; their faces were painted, and they wore garlands round their necks, their *mahouts* (drivers) were handsomely dressed to match. Behind this would follow all the other elephants, in single file, carrying an amazing variety of *howdahs*.

I was once invited to take part in one of these processions, many years later, and sat in an elegantly carved ivory *howdah*, but it felt very rickety, and I feared it might fall to pieces. As I was on the leading elephant of a procession of thirty, I imagined myself being squashed by 120 elephantine feet, and did not enjoy the day as much as I should, although I had pleasant company, a certain Flight Lieutenant Macintyre, the pilot of an expedition to fly over Everest. This was under the command of the Marquess of Clydesdale. The Maharaja had lent them one of his palaces situated in Purnea near the foothills of the Himalayas, as a base, from which they flew in open planes, with no oxygen, taking photographs. This was in the 1930s so no mean achievement in the light aircraft of those days. The procession was in their honour.

I have digressed forward by a score of years and must return to the elephants in my father's care. They were not the easiest of animals, although normally amazingly obedient, there were seasons when the males went *must*, as it was called, getting a discharge from a gland in the side of their foreheads. This caused them to run amok, and one attacked his *mahout* and escaped. He was difficult to recapture, being clever enough to see through all the wiles used. Tranquilliser darts had not been thought of then. He was caught eventually by being encircled by dozens of wooden balls covered in iron spikes. When he found he could not get out of this prickly circle without hurting his feet, nor could he pick them up in his trunk without pain, he gave in by raising his trunk in a salute - a salaam.

My father offered the injured *mahout* another job, but he refused it, insisting on returning to his elephant, who greeted him most affectionately, picking the man up in his trunk and placing him on his back. There was usually a great bond between *mahout* and elephant.

During the 1914-1918 War, things for my father did not change greatly, the fighting never reached Indian shores. He was not called upon for regular service, but remained with the Bihar Light Horse, one of the Territorial units kept in India to be called upon for duty to help the civil power, allowing the regular forces of the British and Indian Army to serve in Europe. After the War, the bottom fell out of the indigo market as synthetic dyes had been introduced. Growing and processing indigo was now profitless, the plants were no longer cultivated, and the simple factories, with their big open drying vats left to moulder.

The Maharaja, in conjunction with a firm of Managing Agents in Calcutta, decided to erect a sugar factory on his land only six miles away from Pandaul. My father was made Manager, and given the job of choosing the site. That part of Bihar is very flat, but extends to the foothills of the Himalayas, where it rises sharply. During the monsoon, the rain is torrential and pours down the mountainous slopes onto the plains with such force that river beds can change their course every few years.

My father needed a river to supply water for the factory, and for drainage, but how to find the right spot on which to build, was his problem. Discovering a portion of a river flowing between an ancient temple, and an enormous old peepul tree, he decided that was the place. It was obvious that that river bed had not altered course in many years. The factory was built nearby and, as far as I know, is still there; to my certain knowledge, it lasted over fifty years at least. Brick bungalows went up for the manager, engineers, chemist, and cane assistants, smaller ones for the Indian clerks, the *babus,* so many more staff were now needed. All were considered luxurious because there was now electricity supplied by the powerful new machinery. I was about five when we moved and had my first sight of electric lights, and the coolness from electric fans.

It must have been wonderful for my mother, who as well as creature comforts had neighbours living within walking distance. Cars had now appeared on the scene, and, as manager of a big concern, my father could afford one, it was a Model T Ford, to me a wonder.

Bihar Light Horse on parade

Another sugar factory was also built about twenty miles away and with the help of cars, small social gatherings became more frequent. White children were in the minority, in fact there were only four of us in the district, none living any nearer than ten miles from each other. We all had to learn to amuse ourselves, but I did have a pony, and rode every day, free to go where I liked as long as a *syce* (groom) ran beside me. It was only a small pony so I do not imagine we went very fast.

I also had my own small plot situated in the vegetable garden, by the well, alongside which was the Head *Mali*'s hut, where he lived.

I was very proud of what I grew and one day when seeing my plants needed water, I went into action. As a result, I learnt about the Hindu caste system. Wanting water, and seeing a potful by the well, I picked it up, it was just what I needed. To my horror, it was snatched away and dashed to the ground, where it shattered. This was done by the Head *Mali* who I had looked upon as a friend and adviser. I stared at him unbelievingly, then saw the fury in his face and ran for the bungalow and my mother. It was impossible for her to explain fully that because of their religion, some Hindus felt that if a non-Hindu touched their food and food vessels, these were now unclean and never to be used again. It was not a question of being rich or poor, but merely the degree of caste into which you were born, you never become a Hindu, you are born one. Both the Maharaja, a millionaire, and the *mali*, who was very poor, were very high caste Brahmins by birth. Our house servants were low-caste, especially the sweeper, and yet they got higher pay than the *mali*, but were looked down upon by him.

The Maharaja entertained non-Hindus lavishly and would sit down at the dining table with them, but he never touched the food he provided, nor did he even eat his own food in front of them. By touching, quite innocently, the *mali*'s pot, I had made it useless to him, and he lost his temper. He was a bit short-tempered, and the house servants did not like him, perhaps because he did look down on them. He was an excellent gardener, which we needed, as we were as self-sufficient as possible, growing an assortment of vegetables and fruit. Among the latter were guavas, bananas, pineapples and Cape gooseberries, also mango and lychee trees. Our farmyard was extensive with chickens and ducks, and I remember turkeys being fattened for Christmas, at which I would whistle to make them gobble at me. At the old Pandaul compound there was even a quail pit. These poor birds had been netted and sold to my father, and were kept in these big pits with a net over it; it sounds so cruel, but they were a great delicacy, and a welcome addition to the usual chicken.

Our milk and butter came from local buffaloes, which my mother insisted on having milked in front of her to ensure its purity, even then it had to be boiled for our good health. Butter made from buffalo milk is very white to Europeans, used to creamy cow butter, it did not look appetising, so it was tinted a pale yellow using the seeds from a shrub growing in the garden producing slightly prickly reddish seed pods. I did not know what it was, merely accepting this as quite normal, therefore never bothered to learn the plant's name.

With a growing European population a Polo club was formed on land near our old Pandaul bungalow, where there was now a new manager installed. No longer was indigo the main crop, now it was sugar cane grown to supply the new factory. He ran the polo which was played once a week and to which all who could came, including the then Maharaja's two young sons, the Kumar Sahibs, nice young men in their late teens, Rameshwar and Viveshvas. They came the twenty miles from Darbhanga by car, usually a Rolls Royce but it was not the same for other young men, working almost as far away. Horses were no problem for them, everyone had a horse, but cars were still only owned by the better off.

If you wanted to play polo you needed two ponies, if you had no car you sent off one pony with its *syce* before dawn. After an early tiffin (lunch) you rode over on your other pony. Your first chukka you played on the pony that had gone ahead and was rested. Your next was played on the pony on which you had ridden over. A third chukka was played on the first pony and your last one on the second pony. Finally you rode home on the pony that had gone ahead, the other plus *syce*, returning at leisure. Complicated and energetic, but that was how it was done. Of course if you were senior enough you drove, giving lifts to as many of those less fortunate as you could.

The cold weather, from the end of October to the end of February, was the factory's busiest time, it was then that the cane was ripe, and full of juice and ready for cutting. During the season work carried on at the factory all the twenty four hours of the day, in eight hour shifts. For the cane assistants, who were responsible for keeping the flow of cane arriving day and night, work never seemed to end, it was not possible for them to keep to steady shifts as in the factory with the cane coming from many small fields within a radius of several miles.

The harvested cane arrived all day by bullock cart, from plots whose owners all wanted their cane cut first. If they could manage to get their fields cleared early in the season, they could plant a second quick crop. Obviously every cane field could not be cleared at once, the factory needed a steady flow throughout the season. The poor cane assistants, who had to regulate this flow as fairly as possible, had difficult choices to make. Not only as to whose cane was cut each day but when the chosen loads got to the factory it all had to be weighed in. Cane needs to be fresh, the longer it lay in the sun, the more it dried out and the less it would weigh; the loss of juice meant less sugar so it was vital to all to get the loads weighed in as quickly as possible. The noise and mle around the weighbridges was like a rugger scrum as each driver tried to get his bullock cart ahead of the others causing a pandemonium of grunts from protesting bullocks, yells from their driver, and the creaking of the carts, causing a dust storm in the process.

When weighed the cane would be thrown on to the conveyor belt which carried it up into the maws of the massive rollers that crushed out the juice, sending it on its way through boilers and centrifuges until it crystallised.

At night the system changed, the cane came from further afield where it was weighed before being loaded into railway wagons, drawn by a little Puffing Billy of an engine along the newly-laid line to the factory. This made for a much quieter process getting it on to the conveyor belt, enabling those living closest to get some sleep at night. Our bungalow was the furthest away so none of this hubbub ever bothered us.

3
Interludes at Home
1920-1932

To go shopping meant a drive of over twenty miles on dirt roads, where you were likely to be held up by a bullock cart trundling along. As there was always a lower road, called a cart leek, available for their use, my father's language on these occasions was mainly unrepeatable. The reasons for these upper and lower roads were twofold, the narrow wooden wheels of the carts cut up the unmetalled surface into such ruts they became impassable to cars. Also for drainage, because in monsoon rains, bullock carts can get through squelchy mud more easily than cars. The Scottish song 'I'll take the high road while ye take the low' was pertinent.

When reaching the town there was not a great deal on offer unless you wanted a new *degchi*, a handleless aluminium cooking pan. These and other pots of many shapes and sizes would be strung up on view, the shiny aluminium catching the eye. Cloth was available, cheap cottons and muslins and it was possible to get khaki drill for the *darzi* to make into Sahib's shorts, also a thinner grey cotton material called *mazri*.

Saris were there in plenty, not the rich silks with their glowing colours, but plain cotton with just a fancy border at the end. The food stalls with their heaped baskets of spices of many pungent kinds were not visited by us. This was Cook's domain.

He did all the shopping for all the local foodstuffs, rice, flour, sugar and so on. Everything else for the household came from Calcutta. Once a month my mother would send off a large order to the Army and Navy Stores there. This would include such things as coffee, quality tea, tins of fruit, sardines, salmon, corned beef, and so on, and for me a tin of boiled sweets out of which she would give me three after tiffin every day. I never knew of chocolates so never missed them. Sadly, now, I cannot open a box without wanting to finish it in one sitting. A crate filled with all our necessities and luxuries would come by train, taking nearly two days, so no perishables were included.

Living like this the arrival of the occasional boxwallah, a travelling salesman was greeted with great excitement. These men travelled all over India, their goods in packs carried by coolies, visiting isolated communities, like ours, and were always welcomed. They would open up their packs, spreading their wares out on the veranda floor.

From Kashmir, in the north, they brought carved wooden articles of all kinds, trays, boxes, table lamps. Out of their loads came also brilliantly painted

13

papier-mâché items, powder bowls and other trinkets. That was not all, intricate embroidery was produced, shawls, and table linen; there followed woollen rugs called numdahs. It was amazing how much and what beautiful objects they carried. To my eyes it was like jewels, and they did good business; being the Manager's wife, my mother got the pick getting first choice before the others as they always came to us first.

Other travelling packmen came from South India, bringing embroidery from various of the Christian missions, cotton tableware and undergarments for ladies. One mission hit on the good idea of sending garments, such as petticoats, knickers, and nighties, cut out and embroidered but not stitched up. This enabled the buyer to have them sewn up to her size. Years later when I came to needing baby clothes they did the same for me. Most birthday and Christmas presents must have come from the boxwallah's packs!

I do not understand why I never had an Indian *ayah*, as was usual, or not that I can recall. I do remember, after our move to the new bungalow, that I did have an Anglo-Indian nurse, called Ethel. I hated her, she had unpleasant ways, the worst of which was to threaten me that if I was naughty, snakes would get me. I still have most vivid memories of waking up at night, imagining snakes completely covering my mosquito net, and slithering all over the floor surrounding my bed. I was sure that if I moved they would get at me. I would be petrified until some night noise would break this terrifying spell. Like many children I never told my parents of this, and still retain a horror of snakes, even the most harmless.

I was about six when my mother's health deteriorated, and Ethel was needed more and more to help her. I never realised why but was just glad to be without her so much.

In 1920 my father was granted Home Leave, he had not been back to Britain since his arrival in India in 1896; my parents had never been away during the ten years of their marriage. There had been occasional jaunts to Calcutta to spend Christmas with my dear Godmother. During the hottest of the hot weather my mother and I might pay visits to a Hill station, like Simla, Darjeeling or Naini Tal, where we might meet my Aunts Eva and Maggie, married to Army officers.

From an early age, I became accustomed to Indian trains, so high off the ground I had to be lifted into the carriages, with their long bunks running down both sides, with windows all the way along. These meant one could watch a wonderful world, never usually seen by me, but the windows themselves fascinated me as they had three frames, one of overlapping slatted wood that shut out the sun, but let in the air, another of fine netting to keep out insects, the third was ordinary glass, and one could decide on which to use.

Always there were the flat plains first, then the lower slopes that were more wooded, into the high hills when the trees gradually changed to conifers. My favourite trip was to Darjeeling, which had such a winding, twisty track, that

14

there were times when one could look out of the window and see both ends of the train at the same time.

After all this, the journey to Bombay was nothing out of the ordinary for me except for being longer than most. The sight of the enormous P & O *SS Nankin* amazed me, used only to the ferry that crossed the Ganges on the way to Calcutta, though by today's standards, she was tiny.

I'd never seen the sea before either, at first it was frightening to have water all round, but by the end of the three week voyage to Tilbury I thought nothing of it.

There another shock awaited me. Until now all white people were Uncles and Aunties, that was how they were known. The Indian gentry that I had met had titles of some kind, the Maharaja was Your Highness, his sons the Kumar Sahibs, a great friend who was a Sikh was Sardarji, the office clerks were Babuji, not that I was really aware then of these niceties. Now I was horrified, looking down from the ship, I saw Uncles carry our luggage like coolies. On board the sailors were lascars, Indians mostly from Bombay and the stewards were Goans, so it hit suddenly.

Worse was to follow because when we got to my English grandmother's house, which must have been a very Victorian establishment, I saw an Auntie sweeping the floor, very upsetting as this was done in India by the very lowest. It must have shaken me considerably because apart from that and the fact I could drink water out of the taps instead of the boiled water from the filter, I can remember nothing of that visit. It is all a blur.

After that we visited my other Grandmother in Northern Ireland, were taken to the seaside with all its wonders, even able to go outdoors shoeless, a thing never allowed in India. I really did get the full sensation of sand between the toes. The sun shone and I was not made to wear a hat. When you have never been allowed out hatless or shoeless, it was quite something. That was a very happy time with a jolly and genuine Aunt, who gave me sweeties to suck in Church, as I was not used to the long boring services, as there had been no Church anywhere near us in India. Being Northern Ireland, Sunday was strictly observed, but the rest of the week was fun. I was sad when the time came to leave, and I never saw my smiling Irish Granny and Aunt Mary again.

When it was time to join the ship back to India, I felt an old hand and had no qualms, little did I realise what my parents might be feeling. My mother must have been seeing doctors while in England, and probably knew she would not see Britain again. To her it was important to be with her husband and child. The normal custom for a child of my age was boarding school, under the care of relatives, but she kept me with her. I did know she was not well because it was my father who saw to my baths. I remember being shocked because in the P&O ships of the time, there were 'Ladies Bathrooms' and 'Gentlemens Bathrooms', and he took me to the 'Gentlemens.'

15

We arrived in Bombay on my seventh birthday and I was told my present would be waiting for me. I was pleased to be back in a world that I understood. I was not surprised to see our Indian bearer there at the dockside in Bombay, awaiting our return. In my child's mind, I probably thought as we had left him there he had been there all the time. Now it seems amazing that these illiterate servants of all the sahibs all over India always managed to be there to greet their employers in this way, no matter how long the journey.

With mounting excitement during the long trip from Bombay to Calcutta, two nights in the train, and then another night from Calcutta to Darbhanga, I longed to see what my birthday present was to be. To my delight, it was a new pony, which had a foal, which trotted along beside us when I went riding. I called them Pauline and Fluff as I was already an avid reader of the children's paper 'The Rainbow' and they were characters in it.

Another change that made me happy was that the hated Ethel was no longer there. Instead there was Miss Naylor, moving in a cloud of the violet perfume she adored, who was to be my governess, another Anglo-Indian, one with elegance, humour, as well as intelligence. I came to like her as much as I had loathed Ethel, and enjoyed my lessons. Life was very pleasant for me.

Not so for my parents, as my mother's health must have been getting worse, but I was not conscious of that, she was always there when I wanted her, with a hand for me to hold and a gentle smile. It was only just over two years since we had returned from England when for some reason unknown to me, Miss Naylor and I were sent to stay with the Chief Engineer and his family, two grown-up daughters whom I admired and were very kind to this little girl. It was a terrible shock when Miss Naylor took me for a walk down to the river, when we had been there only a few days, and told me my mother had died. I could not believe her, turned and ran all the way back to our own bungalow, my father was there on the veranda. I threw myself into his arms, and learnt that it was true. My mother had died early that morning.

Again I was sent away with Miss Naylor to stay much further away, with the family of the manager of another of the Maharaja's estates, which also supplied sugar cane for the factory. He had a daughter a little younger than me, the only other European girl for miles. It was a help to have someone to play with, but without the comfort dear Miss Naylor gave me, I do not know how I could have coped with the grief and the shock. To make matters worse, it was not long after I had returned to a bungalow with my mother no longer there, that I was told I had to go to England because I must go to school. No one would listen when I protested that I would rather stay and go on doing lessons with Miss Naylor.

Before I could really take in what was happening I found myself on board the P & O *RMS Narkunda*, with my father, my godmother, her husband and youngest daughter Angela, four or five years younger than me. I shared a cabin with an American lady, who got very put out when I admitted to not knowing

16

anything about Abraham Lincoln! By then I was well able to bath myself so did not have the indignity of being taken to the men's bathrooms by my father.

Thus ended my childhood days in India. Now it was boarding school, which were not the happiest days of my life. In fact, I hated them, even trying unsuccessfully to run away, luckily for me I did not get very far. After that I realised this was something with which I must put up, as did many other children with parents working in distant lands.

Holidays were spent with various relatives in turn, while I waited for that very special holiday, every other summer when my father would come on leave. When I was about twelve, life became more cheerful because my dear godmother took me over. Her husband had just returned from the Calcutta office of the firm that handled the sugar factory business, he had been transferred to their London office. They bought a big house in Surrey, and had room for me, offering me a home, and my own bedroom, to which I could come back every holiday. It was wonderful. They had four children of their own, Rosamunde, Delicia, Teddy and Angela, of whom I came in the middle. They could have been resentful but instead gave me a happy family life for which I have always been grateful. I have never forgotten their kindness at taking in an outsider and treating me as one of the family. If I had some unhappiness it must have been much worse for my father who had to go back to work, all alone. A sad end to his romantic courtship, winning his bride against all odds, only to lose her for ever after only thirteen years together. He never married again.

R.M.S. NARKUNDA
Pénisulas Oriental Co

1920
We all went back
to India in this
boat.

Return to India 1920

4
To Bihar Again
1932

In 1932, after nine long years of boarding school, which I cannot say I enjoyed, at last it was time for me to return to my father and India. Never was there any idea that I could or should do anything else, but join him in his loneliness. Apart from a course at a school for Domestic Economy, as it was called, where I learnt cooking and the niceties of housekeeping, there was no other more technical training than that. As it turned out this knowledge was useful; I did not have to do any of the chores myself with a houseful of servants but I did know how things should be done. My darling godmother saw I was kitted out correctly for India in the Thirties, with several long evening dresses, complete with long white kid gloves reaching to the elbow, having an opening at the wrist fastened by pearly buttons, enabling the hand to be used when needed. I still have these, and never felt I could discard them, they must almost be museum pieces by now. Another unusual but useful garment was a fancy dress. Fancy dress parties were so popular, my first being on board ship.

Thus at eighteen, a most innocent one, I boarded the BI's *SS Naldera*. I had been kissed but only once because I had given such a smacking response, knowing no better (or perhaps worse) that the young man shied off like a frightened horse. A great disappointment to me because it was such a romantic setting, a moonlight bathing party by the river.

I did learn how I had failed before when taken on the boat deck while we made our way by sea to Calcutta, going ashore at Gibraltar, Malta, Port Said, Aden, Colombo and Madras, a six week voyage, all most exciting. All the same, those kisses on the boat deck with the moon making a silver path over a smooth sea was as far as that went, or was even expected.

I was put in the charge of the most charming Captain I ever met, who had me seated by him at his table. A lady, with two daughters also at his table, took umbrage at this. A mere chit of a girl having this much sought after position instead of a more senior lady like herself, she asked me to change seats with her, and sit with her two daughters. I was happy to oblige.

At the next meal, the Captain asked why I was not sitting beside him, I explained, and was told I was disobeying Captain's orders, and to return to my proper seat, much to the chagrin of the lady concerned when she came in a moment later. I felt so awkward, but I must give her her due, she did not take it out on me as some might have done. Instead she was very kind to me, taking me under her wing so that I got friendly with her daughters and we had some good times together, including shore trips to all the exciting ports I have already mentioned.

Gibraltar Rock, with its apes, and the Almeira Gardens giving me my first sight of bougainvillaea after so many years. Malta, with Valetta Harbour full of the ships of the Fleet, Port Said and the gulli gulli man coming aboard and producing day old chicks out of nowhere. But Colombo has most memories, being taken by rickshaw on my first visit to a Hindu temple, garlands of marigold round my neck, lunch at the Galle Face Hotel, swimming in a little cove nearby and being told afterwards that a shark had been seen there that day.

Madras was a sad day, as we had to say goodbye to the first of our group to leave the ship, a young jockey on his first foreign assignment, who had been great fun. As with many others on that voyage I lost touch for ever.

As normal on these ships there were many young men going out east for their first jobs, almost as green as us girls. We enjoyed ourselves immensely playing deck games, dancing and going ashore in what had been, till now, faraway places with strange sounding names.

At Port Said, wearing topees newly bought from Simon Artz Store, on the way back in 1931 (Joan, aged 18, nearest the camera)

19

My father met me on the ship in Calcutta. When he saw me in the topee (sun helmet), I had bought myself so proudly in Port Said, he was appalled, and ordered me to throw it overboard. He was not going to be seen with me wearing that monstrosity. I had chosen it because it looked like the one I had remembered wearing, a sort of round white mushroom. That was right for a child but was dead wrong now. Instead I was to have a khaki oblong, called a Bombay Bowler. Later I realised how right he had been. My father had his priorities, after the topee was corrected, I must be measured for riding boots and breeches. My godmother had not included these important items. My father obviously thought she had slipped up, forgetting she had lived in Calcutta, not up-country. Once I had my fittings, and the things had been made in the very short time we spent in Calcutta, we set off in the train as in the old days. I was looking forward to being again on the old ferry across the Ganges at Mokameh Ghat only to find it was such a small insignificant vessel, and even the great river not so imposing as I had remembered.

Arriving after a night in transit, at Samastipur Junction, where we had to change trains for the last odd miles of our journey we were met with bad news. The Colonel of the Bihar Light Horse had died the night before, and his funeral was to take place that afternoon. The Indian climate did not allow much time between these events.

As my father was a Captain, and the only officer in this part of Bihar, it was felt he should be present, and so the message had been sent to warn him. I was ensconced in the fresh train while my father checked up on the new arrangements at the station. Before long I realised to my horror the train was moving, then gaining speed. I sat paralysed not even really knowing exactly where in the world I was going. Now I feel cross with myself, this was a chance to pull the communication cord, something I have since so often longed to do but I failed to do it. However there was no need for such action. Soon the train slowed down, then stopped. I looked out to see my father strolling unconcernedly up the track towards me.

Greatly relieved I told him how awful if the train had gone on without him. He laughed. 'You didn't think I'd let that happen surely,' he said. 'But I did,' I replied. 'Of course I told the Station Master to stop it and he had the signals outside the station changed,' he went on.

Our journey continued and we reached Darbhanga station where a car, with my father's uniform well pressed, and his boots and Boer War medals shining with polish, awaited him. As I shall repeat frequently, Indian servants are wonderful. The car took us to the bungalow of the Manager of the Maharaja of Darbhanga, my godfather Gerald Danby, where everyone was to meet for the funeral.

This was a considerable strain, so newly arrived, to have to face all these strange men all at once. It was worse still when they all returned after the ceremony and I was expected to pour out tea for them being the only lady present, since ladies did not attend funerals then. Later, when I met these men again, they expected me to know who they were. 'We've already met' was the refrain when all I had taken in was a crowd of sunburnt faces in khaki uniforms. Much later I heard that when one of these men was asked what the latest girl from Home was like, he said 'Frenchman's idea of a typical English girl.' I was never sure if that was a compliment or not. Eventually, very tired, I arrived at our own bungalow to find my father had been wonderfully thoughtful. He had engaged an *ayah* for me, not the nursery maid type, but one who had been trained as a lady's maid. He had not liked the idea of there being no other woman there.

She was a joy to me, but very bad for my upbringing, as she took complete care of my clothes. In those days it was the done thing always to change into evening dress for dinner, on the dinner jacket in the jungle principle. On going to my room I would find the chosen (by her) dress and etceteras laid out for me. Having to bath in the old tin tub brought me down to earth again. So I lived my lazy life, waited on hand and foot, and I relished it after boarding school. Though I had no work to do, I was active, riding every morning before breakfast on the magnificent 15-hand Australian waler my father had bought for me, called Cavalier, a beautiful chestnut horse. No longer did I have a *syce* running beside me, he could never have kept up anyway.

I ranged for miles round the countryside through the little villages with evocative smells, that of the mustard oil in which the food was cooked, and the scent of the cow dung used for fuel. That does not sound a pleasant mixture, but it has a strange nostalgic aroma for me. I rode past their small thatch houses, with their mud floors so clean with constant sweeping, renewed when necessary by another layer of muddy paste smoothed on with careful hands.

Wood was scarce in north Bihar, so unlike Assam, as I was to find out many years later. Permission from the Sub-Divisional officer was needed to cut down a tree, hence the dung fires. There were even law suits over the ownership of a single tree.

I rode through mango groves, past clumps of bamboos, along the little banks of earth that surrounded each small field, retaining the water when the monsoon came, thus to help rice cultivation. During the dry season a kind of pea was grown. There were the larger plots of sugar cane, blocking the view, having to be ridden around, much too thick to ride through. I got to know every little track, the villagers got to know me, smiling as I passed and it gave me a lasting love of that country.

I can remember only one fall when a pi-dog in a village caused my horse to shy, and I went over his head, but landed with the reins in my hand, as I had been taught. The villagers gathered round very concerned, while I sat there in the dust. Was I all right ? 'Tik hai? Tik hai?' they asked. I assured them I was, mounted my horse, thanked them and rode home.

The only area I came to dislike was the ruins of an old indigo factory, a branch of the main Pandaul one that had been abandoned even before my father's time there. I once got off my horse to examine the place.

Immediately I found myself becoming surrounded by monkeys, quickly getting back on to my horse to get away from them, we had to make our way through trees, from which more monkeys were descending. By now both Cavalier and I were equally frightened because as he tried to gallop away, there were monkeys all round us. Thankfully some men working in fields nearby saw what was happening and ran towards us, brandishing sticks and yelling which scared off the monkeys, and they scurried back up the trees, leaving Cavalier and me to get away. Sadly I never had money on me as I would have liked to reward these men, all I could do was try and thank them.

My days were spent enjoyably, a ride first thing, then possibly a round of golf on the new 9-hole course, followed perhaps by tennis in the afternoon, and sometimes ending the day with a game of bridge. The system of shifts suited me well because it meant there was usually someone ready to join me for most of these activities. It was pleasant after years of boarding school to be so free to play all day.

The golf course, though small, was quite tricky, being bordered by the river on one side. The greens had to be protected from grazing buffaloes by iron posts in the corners with wire running round. My greatest success was a hole in two, achieved by a drive so wild it hit the corrugated iron roof of a servants' quarter in an adjacent compound. It bounced back well up the fairway. My iron shot hit the post on the furthest corner of the green and should have carried on till it ended in the river. Instead it rocketed back into the hole. A birdie!

My father always held open house for tennis on Sunday afternoons. He was particularly proud of his two courts, planted with a special kind of grass, known as *doop*. This was a low spreading type, and was planted by cut pieces of it mixed with mud and water into a thick paste; this was spread by hand and left to grow until established enough to mow. The ordinary grass was too stiff and coarse.

Saturday afternoons were sacred. No one stirred from their bungalows unless they had to. Callers were unwelcome. This was the day the Home Mail arrived with wonderful regularity, taking three weeks on the way; travelling by train across France to Marseilles, there catching the P & O liner to Bombay. Thence by train again to Calcutta, and on to us up-country. You knew that you would get your letters from Home, magazines and newspapers, the latter being bound weekly editions. So Saturday afternoon was dedicated to catching up on news from Home, and it must have been the same for many all over India. The arrival of the latest book was a real joy to everybody as the contents of neighbours' bookcases were exhausted. A new record for our wind-up-gramophone was cause for celebration. If anyone came back from Home leave without bringing fresh books and records, their name was mud, since we were so starved of fresh reading and music. The wireless was not a great help, the output was poor and the signals too weak.

I had arrived in India in mid-October, the beginning of the cold weather, and by November, invitations poured in to stay with my father's friends in other areas, particularly for Meets. The first I went to was the Muzaffarpur Meet, the event at which my parents first met. I did not do as they had done and fall in love, but did not lack for partners at the dances, or the games; girls were at such a premium.

Not only I, but my horse with his *syce* went too, travelling by train in a horse box for the seventy miles. This was customary, and mine was not the only horse that attended. Mounted gymkhanas were always featured, and there was polo, of course, but not for ladies, not yet. On occasions I remember going home from a dance changing into riding kit and off for a dawn ride.

One of the invitations I received was from the Raja of Hathwa, a minor princeling, the gentleman that I looked upon as our Maharaja was the Maharajadhiraj of Darbhanga, to give him his full title. He was the most important locally, although not a ruling prince, but he was of exceedingly high caste as well as being one of the richest men in India.

It was he, and his younger brother, I had known so well as a child when they were learning to play polo. Now he had ascended to the *gaddi*, the throne, in his late uncle's place. There was a strange superstition that no Maharaja of Darbhanga ever had a son, it was always his brother's son who inherited. Certainly this Maharaja had none, but was treating his nephew as his heir. There were many petty Rajas, whose titles were really only honorary, and the Raja of Hathwa was one of these, a very hospitable and generous man, who enjoyed having house parties. It was to one of these I was invited. He had a special guest house, like a small palace, in which I and the other guests stayed. All the usual entertainments were laid on, such as polo and tennis, with a *nautch* in the evening. This was an Indian dance troupe, accompanied by musicians and singers. At first the Indian music had no appeal for me, it needs understanding, but I grew to like it. I definitely prefer it to a lot of the music of the present time. Sadly the chief memory of that is a feeling of embarrassment.

All the ladies of our party were invited to tea with the Rani, and the ladies who lived in purdah in the zenana, the ladies' quarters of the palace. They never met any man other than those of their immediate family. They were able to watch some events behind a tracery in certain rooms and balconies. Not surprisingly they spoke no English, and why should they, in their rainbow-like saris, worn so elegantly, they looked like a flock of birds, but birds in golden cages. Compared with them our clothes were so dull, straight, sleeveless cotton frocks without any glamour.

Protocol demanded that the senior British lady, the Commissioner's wife was the one to introduce our party; and to make conversation with the Rani.

Unfortunately she could speak little or no Hindi, all she seemed capable of were phrases such as 'Tik hai' meaning 'all right', in varying inflections to indicate a question or a fact. Tik hai? Tik hai!

As the least important member of our party I stayed in the background, covered in shame while the poor Rani endeavoured to understand her guest. I vowed then that I would learn to speak Hindi as fluently as I could.

In his usual way my father came up trumps, engaging a *munshi*, a teacher for me, so I spent several mornings a week learning to speak Hindi. This had mixed results because my tutor spoke high class Hindi, most suitable for chatting up Ranis; but I needed to speak to our servants and local villagers, picking up the common '*bat*' or talk. As in France with 'tu' or 'vous' it was 'tum' or 'aap'. I did not always get it right, exact pronunciation was important, and I did get mixed up sometimes. Calling up the *bawarchee*, the cook, and the *khansamah*, the butler, I gave my orders for a dinner party for twelve. I went through the menu in great detail, and was sure they both knew what was needed. On the morning of the party I did my best floral arrangement for the table, not letting the mali do the flowers as usual.

The guests having arrived I thought I would just check the table was correctly laid, I looked into the dining room. Imagine my horror to discover only two places laid instead of twelve! Feeling like screaming but knowing I must restrain myself, I called for the *khansamah*, demanding an explanation.

'Miss Sahib', you ordered a big dinner, a *burra khana*, of many dishes. Cook has done as you said.'

'There are only two places!' I said. 'I asked for dinner for twelve, *bara* for *khana*.' (Twelve for dinner). Then I realised I had confused *BARA* meaning twelve with *BURRA* meaning big. I had asked for a big dinner, not one for twelve and that was what had been done.

However Indian servants could always rise to the occasion, dinner was somewhat delayed, and we 'killed tins' as the expression was, and with Cook's ingenuity a good dinner was served.

Having taken my father aside to explain the delay quietly, I was taken aback when he roared with laughter and told everybody this 'big' joke. That is the story of my very first dinner party.

Not only was my father manager of the new sugar factory, he was also an Honorary Magistrate for our local Sub-Division of Madhubani. There was a young sub-divisional officer, newly out from Britain on his first posting in the Indian Civil Service, who often asked my father for advice. There was one imponderable case! In one of the villages there was a mixture of Hindus and Muslims as was often the way. A big banyan tree grew there, considered holy by the Hindus. Nearby was a Muslim graveyard, once the two had been far apart. As the years passed the banyan tree grew bigger, its branches spreading further. Likewise as more died and were buried, the graveyard grew also. A peaceful village became an angry one as the Hindus blamed the Muslims for encroaching under the sacred tree, while the Muslims said the shade of the tree was desecrating their graves.

The case was passed to my father to judge. He suggested they lop a few boughs off the tree and dig up the nearest graves to be fair to both sides, but that did not please either side.

My father then told them that, as a Christian himself, he should not advise in this religious matter. He advised them to get counselling from the holiest and wisest men of both sects, let them come to the village and consider the case. The villagers were delighted at the idea, but asked how this could be done. My father suggested that a letter should be written to Benares, the holiest Hindu city, and another to Lucknow where there was a learned Muslim community, asking for scholars of both places to visit and make a decision. Then he pointed out that they would have to pay the rail fares, First Class, for such important men. Also it would be necessary to feed them for the entire time it took them to settle the difficulty. Such eminent persons would expect the best food for an unknown period. When my father asked if they would like him to write the letters, there was silence, so he told them to go away and think about it among themselves. He never heard anything more, and the villagers were at peace with each other.

5
Servants & Snakes

Indian servants cannot receive too much praise from me, I admire their faithfulness, and their ability to cope with all situations. They have done so much for me over many years, and my thanks are due to them for making my life easy in strange and difficult situations, all through my time in India. I do not think I appreciated all they did, while they were doing it, I simply accepted it all. How did the cooks produce such superb dishes with poor ingredients, dreadful kitchens and the most primitive of cookers? The kitchens were separated from the bungalows presumably so no odours could penetrate, so how did the servants manage to serve up the food so elegantly, when having to carry it in through monsoon storms? How did they do that and keep their uniforms so spotless and white? How did the *dhobies* (the washermen) deliver such white starched shirts after beating them on stones by muddy river banks? I will never know.

The first stove I saw was when I joined my father after school. There in the kitchen I found a mud plastered edifice, with an opening for a fire low down, above which were holes on which stood the *degchies*, or pots. Because the factory used coal, that was used, but it must have been difficult to regulate the heat. Remember, too, they were not cooking their kind of food, but European dishes completely foreign to them, and which they did not eat themselves, and yet a Muslim cook would still get the breakfast bacon just right, boil the Christmas ham to perfection, and make the most delectable ham souffle with the remains. The bacon and ham were specially ordered from Darjeeling in the winter. The cook may never have seen either in his youth, and would certainly never eat it, or any other form of pork.

Their pastry was a wonder, especially when you consider that the flour used had to be sieved to remove the weevils, and if it was a sweet one then the sugar might have had to be de-anted first. The refrigerator, which we did have, now electricity was available to us, had its legs standing in tins of water, as did the kitchen cupboards and tables to keep out ant and cockroach invasions. None of this ever bothered me, I suppose because I'd seen it all as a child.

Servants always did their best to please as in the case of the sahib who tended to fall asleep during dinner. He was partial to a fresh cooked snipe, and whenever he woke up a piping hot snipe would be placed before him. Unbelievable this may seem but it is true, because I knew the sahib in question. Snipe were plentiful in the cold weather, and he did find his cook's bill then rather high. He supposed a succession must have been cooked, and he appreciated his cook's efforts to please.

At a dinner party to which I went, the mashed potato was coloured bright pink. Judging by the hostess' expression, this was a surprise to her, but was obviously an effort to make it special for a party. The first time I went to dinner with one of the young assistants I was surprised to see that most of the crockery and cutlery used, including a rather special dessert service, were my father's. I was indignant but said nothing until on the way home, when I told my father our servants must be spoken to about this. His things should not be borrowed like this. He told me not to interfere with normal custom. These young men did not yet own more than their basic needs, but their servants wanted to put on a good show for prestige, so all the servants collaborated. My father, the Burra Sahib, had the most so his were borrowed. The Chota Sahib probably knew nothing about this arrangement. All the same I did beg, and my father agreed, that his precious and fragile dessert service should not wander like this. The servants were told, and it never appeared on any other table again, although many of his other things did. I still have the set.

People sometimes ask about snakes, of which, as I have explained, I have a dread, also about creepy crawlies in general, shuddering perhaps as they ask. I have to admit that I myself have no horror stories to tell them. My dear godmother did warn me, before I returned to India, that I should always shake out my shoes before I put them on, and for a while I did. In spite of my mindless fear of snakes from my childhood nightmares, they never harmed me.

Those poor, who are forced to sleep on the floor, are at risk. A snake might crawl onto a limb for warmth, if the sleeper moved the snake could react in fright and bite. There were a lot of deaths from snake bites reported from villages, but my father did not believe all were genuine, but were cases of murder by poison. No autopsies were done in those outlying places. The shoeless could easily step on a sleeping snake, but usually a snake will try and get out of the way first.

There was the case of the servant of a planter, Bill, who came running to him one day in a panic, yelling that he had been bitten by a snake when he was on his way to work. Bill examined his foot, but could see no sign of a bite. He got a magnifying glass but still could see no punctures. The other servants were told to look and all agreed there was no sign of a bite. Still the man insisted he had been bitten and had seen the snake strike. Trying to reassure him, Bill said it must have been so drowsy it struck out but had not bitten so he was in no danger. Since the man was so fearful Bill said he could have the day off and go home. Next morning the man did not appear for work, so someone went to his house and heard the man was dead. On hearing this, Bill called all the other servants together, pointing out they had seen no mark, so the man could not have been bitten.

That was the trouble, he was told, it must have been a ghost snake not to have left any traces. If it had been a normal snake they were sure the sahib could have cut out the poison and treated it with medicine and all would have been well.

With a ghost snake nothing could be done, and they had told the man so. He went home and died of fright.

The bungalows of our community connected with the sugar factory were not far apart, so visiting was on foot. If darkness fell while we were out, a servant with a lantern, the good old *haathbati*, would come to light his sahib home, walking in front. After a big party there would be quite a gathering of servants with lamps, which must have helped the heavy drinkers.

One evening my father, and cane manager, were walking up the path to our bungalow, it was just dusk so no lamp was needed, as they thought, when my father called 'Look out, there's a snake on the path.' 'Rubbish,' said the other, 'that's not a snake' and proceeded to kick it all the way till the light from the veranda showed it was a cobra. The snake slithered away probably in a state of shock.

The cobra is usually held in greatest awe, but the one to fear most is the krait. The cobra needs to rear up a third of its length to strike. The krait can dart, being thin and dark, and not much longer than a foot, it can hide, and strike with great agility. It can slide through the drainage pipe of the bathrooms, even get on to the tops of doors and drop on the unwary. Thank goodness this did not happen to me, but I did hear of it.

My father gave me a mongoose as a pet, friendly creatures but not cuddly, but renowned as killers of snakes, as anyone who has read Rudyard Kipling's 'Rikki Tikki Tavi' will know. Mine was called Bijli which is Hindi for both lightning and electricity , a suitable name since he was so quick. I had great faith in his ability to protect me from snakes. My faith was justified, but there was a moment when I doubted.

Our beds were made of wooden frames with a lattice of *newar*, a broad woven tape about three inches wide, woven across over and under so that there was a space the width of the wooden frame between the two layers of *newar*.

Over that would go the mattress, with a mosquito net hanging from a frame held up by the bed poles, and tucked under the mattress. It was much wiser to tuck it in than leave it hanging to the ground as seen in many films of the tropics. In the middle of the night I was woken by a wriggling under the mattress, my immediate thought was 'a snake' and yelled to my father who slept in the next room. 'Keep still,' he called back, 'I'll get my gun.' In he came, gun at the ready. 'Jump out quickly,' he ordered. I did. Nothing happened. He handed me the gun, and, bravely, pulled off the bedding. Out popped Bijli, surprised at having his nap disturbed.

Although so friendly Bijli could be naughty. Once when we had a dinner party, I heard strange tinkling sounds coming from the dining room. On investigation, I caught Bijli rolling glasses off the table and listening, ears cocked, to the sound they made crashing on the stone floor. Bijli got on well with our other pets, a basset hound and a cat. The basset was very greedy and always hoped to be first at the food. This was always shown to one of us by the sweeper, who then put it down by the doorway to the veranda. The animals knew the drill, Bertie Basset stood ready, nose at the crack of the double doors, nudging the others away but never got there first. Cinders, the cat, leapt over his back, Bijli slipped underneath, but he never gave up trying. Sadly Bertie was run over in our drive when we were away on leave, and someone was acting in place of my father. Bijli's great treat was a raw egg, he would sit up on his back legs holding it very delicately in his front paws and nibble and suck into it. He was a great joy to me, both friendly and mischievous.

6
Calcutta - Balls & Races
1933

Signs of the hot weather became evident. All the sugar cane was cut, teams of buffalo were busy ploughing up the fields before the monsoon made this all but impossible. Hot west winds made stepping out of doors like entering a modern fan oven set on high. The cotton trees, with their scarlet blooms flowered overhead. The landscape became yellower, drier and dustier daily. In the factory the machinery was being overhauled by sweating mechanics. I chose then to come down with a virulent attack of dengue fever, which makes every part of the body ache almost unbearably and takes its time to wear off. I was more than glad to know that my father's home leave was almost due, as at that moment I was not enjoying life in India.

I did enjoy the long train journey across India to Bombay. Although I had made the journey three times before, it had been as a child, accepting without question all that I saw as a part of India and normal life. Now I found it absorbing, lolling on my bunk in the railway carriage with a panorama flowing past outside. The countryside altering as the train traversed the different regions. Variations in the people, their dress, houses, and cultivations depending on whether we were in flat plains, thick jungle areas, or hill slopes. Very distinct were the moments when we crossed rivers on great metal bridges echoing like thunder around us, as the iron girders of their sides rumbled past. All this was broken at intervals by a steamy rush into stations. There bustle, noise and hubbub were all around. People jostling to board the train oblivious of those trying to get off. Coolies vying to grab the luggage of descending passengers, especially from First Class carriages.

Men selling tea in little earthenware cups calling their wares 'Garam chai, garam chai' (Hot tea). Others with screws of paper holding nuts crying 'Chini Badam', others with *paans* in cornets of banana leaves, made their wares known. Behind this was the mixed smell of spices, smoke and sweat, pervading all, leaving a mixed impression of heaven and hell.

The journey was never dull, but it was hot, the month being June. With the Mail train there was a restaurant car, in and out of which we climbed at suitable stations, finding the cutlery too hot to handle without a napkin to hold it by. When I said 'climbed' I meant it, as there were three tiers of steps, one directly above the other to get into the high carriage.

The First Class compartments in which we travelled had a long bunk on each side, with another bunk above, which was folded up in daytime, this was

30

for four passengers and had its own toilet, with basin and loo. Fans whirled but did little when it was really hot to cool the air. Calcutta to Bombay took two nights, everyone travelled with their own bearer and their own bedding, which the bearer laid out at night. Attached to the First Class carriages would be one for bearers to give them easy access to their sahibs.

On board ship was great fun, as ever, but the P & O *SS Rawalpindi* was a lot bigger than the BI liner in which I had gone out to Calcutta. *Rawalpindi* was one of the fleet of liners in which the P & O carried the mail every week out from England via the many ports on the way either to China or Australia and back again. Sadly she was sunk in action during the 1939/45 War, with a friend of mine on board; I am glad to say he was one of the lucky survivors. There was more in the way of entertainment, even films which were a treat as I only saw them on my visit to Calcutta. I enjoyed it so much that I was sorry it only took two weeks.

My father always disembarked at Marseilles, going across France in the then famous Blue Train. This cut out a week of sailing, and the Bay of Biscay, noted for its bad weather. For our return journey I begged to be allowed to do the whole voyage by sea, so I embarked at Tilbury while he joined the ship at Marseilles as usual.

During the next cold weather my father decided a spell away in Calcutta would be a good idea, so just after my twentieth birthday, I went to stay with a young couple; he worked in the firm which dealt with all the factory business as Managing Agents. A delightful pair, his being a junior post they were glad of a paying guest. My father was happy to arrange this because I had just declined the attentions I had been receiving from his Chief Engineer in favour of a handsome, newly joined assistant engineer. Getting rid of me for a while was the best way out of an awkward situation, especially as the Chief Engineer had just proposed.

I had a wonderful time in Calcutta. While I was there the Viceroy of India, Lord Willingdon, was residing in his Calcutta residence, Belvedere, and he decided to have an Historical Ball. Most of the year he and Lady Willingdon lived in Delhi, this was an opportunity to entertain residents of Calcutta. This event became known as the Hysterical Ball, by the less dignified folk in Calcutta as some people seemed to go quite mad over their costumes.

For the well off, a costume was no problem, with all the gorgeous silks, and wonderful embroidery available in Calcutta, not to mention most excellent tailors who could work from pictures, and Chinese shoemakers who evolved shoes of all colours and shapes. Elegant wigs were produced, embroidered gloves, everything that any exquisite might have worn at the Sun King's Court at Versailles was available, if you had the money and the imagination. The Viceregal party came as the Court of King Charles I, with Lord Willingdon as the King, who he did indeed resemble. Lady Willingdon was Queen Henrietta Maria, and the *aides-de-camp* and the attachés, were the courtiers.

I had no problem as I had my faithful old fancy dress, which happened to be a Dolly Varden so counted as historical. The couple I was staying with, with

31

their special friends, were not in a position to afford massive expenditure. Also they objected to this flaunting of flummery for a single evening. They decided to go as Anglo-Saxons, which was an historical period. They wore the roughest cloth tunics, with hessian tied round their legs and feet and round aluminium bowls from the bazaar with buffalo horns attached on their heads. They got several disapproving looks, but we all thoroughly enjoyed ourselves; I'd have liked to go as one of them but I could not even spare that many rupees from my dress allowance, there were so many other things I wanted more. It was a wonderful spectacle like a fairy tale ball, an evening I shall not forget. It was an exciting visit all round, the Maharaja of Darbhanga was also visiting Calcutta then and heard I was there, so he invited me to come to the Races. The Calcutta Races were an important part of the social scene, with jockeys from Britain, excellent horses, many from Australia, and a fine building, and course.

Everything was done by Jockey Club rules. The Maharaja had his own box, and his Secretary was sent off to do our betting. Although so rich he was very peevish as he lost a small amount, while I won ten rupees, a godsend to me. I also managed to get some riding on a horse lent me by a young Cavalry officer stationed there. The only place convenient to reach was a *maidan*, a park-like stretch adjoining a tennis club, and not too far from his lines. I had some pleasant rides in this young man's company until the day when a badly hit tennis ball struck my horse as we cantered past the courts. Not surprisingly I came off. Many of the tennis players came running out to see if I was all right, which was most embarrassing. My escort was more anxious about the horse. We never went riding again.

On my return back up-country, I steered clear as far as was possible in such a small community, from both the engineers, much to my father's relief. There was a young cane assistant on the other sugar factory in the area, with whom I found more in common, we both liked the latest jazz records and I arranged for a selection to be sent on approval from Calcutta; Bill was in camp at that time organising the cane for the factory for which he worked. My father let me have the car to take the latest batches over to Bill where we could try them out on his portable gramophone. Long after I asked my father how he could let me go off to spend the day in a young man's tent. 'I trusted you both not to let me down,' he said, and we didn't.

7

Bihar Earthquake

1934

Early the following hot weather, my father got ill with jaundice during a business trip to Calcutta to see the Managing Agents. I was thankful this had happened where he could get proper medical treatment, as the facilities locally were distant and poor. A gallstone was diagnosed, needing an operation. It was decided that he should go to England for this. Meanwhile, he was to take a spoonful of olive oil with every meal, which he did. We arrived in Britain in May, in a snowstorm, something we had not expected, and very different from the heat we had left behind. My father visited the London specialists, who ignored the X-rays he had with him, taken in Calcutta, which was just as well, because the new X-rays showed no sign at all of any gallstones. No operation was needed. It is my firm belief that the olive oil dissolved the gallstone.

However, the serious side of all this made me realise what an utterly useless person I was. I was nearly twenty-one, with no training for any thing. Obviously, my father's retirement was looming nearer, and I had better learn to do something useful. There was little scope for someone who had had an expensive education, but had only a school certificate to show for it, had been good at games and in demand to play for the honour of the House, very Angela Brazil-like. The only possibility was to learn typing and shorthand, so that is what I did. Touch typing came easily, but the shorthand was hard. My lazy life, with little use of my brain, made learning difficult. It did not help me to gain proficiency when the course had to be cut short.

Since, fortunately for my father, he did not need an operation, he must return to India sooner than expected. There was never any question that I should not accompany him, and I expected to do so; he had had so many lonely years after my mother's death, and he had done so much for me. That was the first voyage on which I had a yearning for true romance. Till then, my mild flirtations had meant little. This time I fell for a dashing squadron leader in the Fleet Air Arm, on his way to join *Ark Royal* in Hong Kong, so much more exciting than planters. Sadly, I had a rival, and she was going all the way to Singapore!

I felt very jealous! He was sweet to both of us, though we must have been a trial to him. Bombay was reached far too soon, my only consolation being that he did come to the train, and kissed me goodbye, and he was still single when he arrived in Hong Kong. For a while we corresponded, and he sent me clever sketches he had done of characters on board. I never saw him again, but did check up years later that he had survived the War.

33

On our return, my father agreed that I could come to his office in the mornings, and type his personal correspondence. Unfortunately, the *babus* (clerks) there did not like my presence. They were always most polite, but obstructive. The paper, the envelopes, the carbons, were never handy for me, and I could feel their resentment. When invitations to Meets from all over Bihar poured in since it was the beginning of the cold weather, my efforts at being a good private secretary wilted under the pressure. It seemed pointless, when my services were not really needed, so I continued my frivolous life to the end of 1933. The year 1934 was to bring something quite different.

A frightening day for us was 15th January 1934, at 2.13pm; the day of the Bihar earthquake. Fortunately this event occurred in the daytime, during siesta time for my father and me. Lying on my bed, luckily fully clad, I heard a rumbling. It sounded like the Northwester that usually heralded the monsoon, but this was January! Rapidly the sound grew louder, and louder still, a giant express train nearing, then the first shock waves hit. My bed rocked, and I leapt off and tore out of my room, but it was difficult to run as the floor behaved like a roller coaster, up one moment and down the next. With difficulty I stumbled across the veranda, tumbling down the steps into the garden, urged on by my father's yells. The lawn was behaving like a billowing sea, great waves instead of flat grass. Two cars, parked outside the garage, were rolling backwards and forwards in unison, partners in a formal dance, brakes were often forgotten in such a flat area. As I gazed at them, the ground under my feet cracked open, splits appeared around me, and out of these spouted high gushers of hot liquid, a muddy mixture. Having been given a Rolleiflex camera by my father at the very recent Christmas, I felt I must capture this astounding sight. All fear left me and I dashed back into the bungalow to get it, in spite of loud protests from my father.

Sadly, during this time the spouts had lost their force, subsiding into foot high gushers pouring out this warm brownish water. I took my photos, though had not got the spectacular ones I'd hoped for, but I still have my record of that day and of how our garden looked under about three feet of dirty sand. I was never able to cash in on these pictures because, cut off as we were for many days, there was no way I could get them developed, let alone printed or sent to newspapers. All this seemed to have taken a long time, but when I learnt of the seismograph record later on it was only two and a half minutes, but I understand that this is quite long in earthquake terms. The garden became unrecognisable under a coating of a mixture of mud, sand and water.

My father's first thought was for the factory, then in full production. That it was still standing we could still see, but in what state? He took off immediately, leaving me to take my photos. We were incredibly lucky, not one person was killed or badly injured, the only casualty was a man scalded by steam from the boilers. The massive flywheel, weighing tons, whirling round at many revolutions per minute, remained intact, but at an angle of 45 degrees. If that had got

Earthquake photo! Three feet of warm watery sand covering the lawn

loose it would have sliced its way through the whole mill, causing terrible damage and probably deaths. The hero of the day was the *tindal mistri*, the head boilerman, who immediately drew the fires from all the big boilers, thus saving them from blowing up, and causing devastation. He then ran away and was not seen again for weeks, but he had saved the factory.

The wonder of that day was due to the timing of the quake at 2.13 in the afternoon. There was an exceedingly long brick building used for stacking the sacks of sugar on production. It had only one door in its entire length. Through this door coolies bore the bags of newly-produced sugar, eventually carrying it all out again to be taken to market by the little Puffing Billy engine and its wagons. Normally, a long line of men, loads on their backs, would be carrying these either in or out of the godown, or store. Manpower was much cheaper than automation. Luckily at 2.00pm the old shift was coming off duty while the new one was still signing on, or, more likely, giving their thumb prints. The building collapsed like a pack of cards. No one inside could have survived, but no one was there.

If anyone was hurt at all, it was in the stampede out of the mill yard to get home. Their houses, being made of bamboo, thatch, and perhaps mud walls did not suffer as did those of brick. Before long the mill yard was awash with this muddy broth left by the gushers when their flow subsided. Because it was impossible to see the wells of the turnpits for the engine, some staff did fall in. The main building still stood, the pans of boiling syrup held in place. Being constructed mainly of iron girders, and corrugated iron sheets these must have merely swayed.

Soon darkness fell with the quick descent of nightfall in the East. The workforce, sensibly, had fled to their houses, and were in no danger. The British staff were not so fortunate, most of their brick-built bungalows were wrecked, ours was in the best condition. Being on slightly higher ground, the liquid round it had not reached above the plinth on which it was built. My father offered hospitality to all, and since our cookhouse was undamaged, our servants set to in their inimitable way to prepare dinner for everyone, even down to after-dinner coffee.

Unfortunately, that was when the second shake hit us. This really shook me, as well as everything around. Between me and the door was a high-backed wooden settee. I cleared it in one bound, not caring a hoot that I held one of my father's best coffee cups. He lost most of his beautiful service that evening. That brought realisation that even our bungalow was not a safe place in which to sleep. The roof of the long veranda had begun to fall away from the main building. All available beds were collected and lined up between bungalow and cookhouse, one of the very few patches of ground not a marsh. They looked like small tents with their white mosquito nets giving a parade ground effect. Of course, there was no electricity, which the factory normally generated, but there was no shortage of hurricane lamps. It was not a peaceful night from then on, as the after-shocks had started. These smaller shakes continued to hit us for several weeks, always catching us by surprise.

Next day was spent trying to create some order out of chaos. Not a lot could be done in the factory, bar inspections. It was still awash, and no labour had turned up. Not very surprising. The main machinery was still intact, but at an acute angle. My father told me later that his most frightening moment had been when he, as Manager, had climbed up to the high pan floor where the syrup from the crushed cane was boiled, then drained down to the centrifugals where it was crystallised before being fed down chutes and bagged. Wondering if the whole floor would tilt over and collapse in a mess of sticky syrup, he knew he must check it before letting anyone else up to examine the structure.

It was later found that only our particular area had suffered from this flooding from underground. It may have been because we were nearest to the Himalayas, the pressure of their weight forcing up the water, or perhaps because we were near a big river. The quake had extended on for a hundred miles, causing great cracks and fissures in the ground, and considerable damage everywhere. We were entirely cut off, our radio, worked by electricity, was useless, and we had no idea what was happening elsewhere. The railway line looked like a writhing snake, the roads and bridges were twisted and unusable. Until someone thought of riding, we had no news, the nearest town was twenty miles away. The young engineer who had offered to go found all the roads, bridges, and railway lines in the same bad way as ours. Villages had not suffered as much, and were able to look after themselves. When he got to the town it was heaps of rubble, but the telegraph had got going. He then discovered that the shake had extended for about one hundred miles.

With labour abundant, men with shovels were soon digging away, and the women carrying baskets of earth away on their heads. Taking it to where it was needed, soon the roads were made passable, and with bamboo structures for bridges.

Because it happened in the afternoon, there were few deaths, people had been able to escape before the buildings fell, unlike the Quetta earthquake a couple of years later, which happened in the middle of the night. The old bungalow, where I had been born, collapsed completely, and the manager and his wife only just escaping, the bedroom wall falling behind them as they reached the veranda, a deep double one that also fell as they passed through it. They had all the company equipment for touring, so were able to make themselves comfortable. Neither they nor any of our community had children to worry about. That's enough about this earthquake, except that I do realise how incredibly lucky we were.

8

To Kashmir
(for hot weather - 1934)

The moment full assessment could be made of the damage, and of the requirements my father became particularly busy. He did not know what effect the monsoon would have. What would the river do when in full spate? How would the ground react after the recent upheaval? I was not going to be much help, so plans were made for me to spend the 'hot weather' in Kashmir. An Army officer's widow took in paying guests on her houseboat on the river Jhelum in Srinagar, and she agreed to have me.

To get to Srinagar, I had to travel three days and two nights by train across India, a prospect that was too much for my Darjeeling-born *ayah*, the width of India between there and home, especially after the trauma of the earthquake. She left for home, and I did not try to persuade her to stay. I could now speak the language, and was well able to look after myself, but I did appreciate the help she had been when I had first arrived from my English school. All the same, it was simply not done for me to travel all alone. In fact, bearers always accompanied their sahibs on trains, with special compartments adjoining the First Class coaches.

I believe trains were the biggest boon the British brought to India. Indians always seemed to be enjoying travelling on them. The rich with their servants and piles of luggage, the poor crowding close packed as sardines in the sparsely furnished Third Class carriages, clinging even to the doors, or sitting on the roof, the middle class in the privacy of the smaller Second Class coupés. The load those trains carried must have been enormous, far beyond the imagination of the manufacturers, but they fulfilled all that had been asked of them.

I had recently acquired a cocker spaniel puppy, born during all the pandemonium of the earthquake, and the only survivor of his litter. He was black, with a V-shaped white shirtfront. The obvious name was Quaker, and that was it.

I set off with my father's most trustworthy and experienced bearer, who had been with him before I was born. I was told that I would crawl to him and haul myself to my feet, hanging on to his legs, and he put up with this baby very patiently. With us went Quaker. Indian Railways had a rule that ladies travelling alone could have a dog in the carriage with them for protection. Quaker fulfilled this qualification, though only four months old. He could never have stood the guards van, which was the alternative; he felt the heat so much.

It was mid-May when we set off, and really hot. By telegraphing down the railway line ahead I was able to order a large metal container with a block of ice

38

about 2'x 1' x 1' for my compartment. By directing the overhead fan on to this, and tying a wet towel under it, one was able to reduce the heat a little. Also, I was able to chip off slivers of ice for Quaker to lick. This was not a journey by a mail train which had a restaurant car, but by sending messages ahead to certain stations, a meal on a tray could be handed in to one's carriage. The tray and used crockery was passed out at the next station at which we stopped. It would then be returned by another train, an admirable arrangement, which worked beautifully, even including some meat and rice for Quaker. We had to change trains twice, and while Daroga, the bearer, dealt capably with my luggage, I would walk with Quaker as far as I could out of the station. The important part of the luggage was always the bedding roll, or *bistra*, laid out at night, and rolled up in the day. Trains then did not supply bedding.

Eventually, we reached Rawalpindi, the railhead, where I spent the night in a hotel, and was able to revel in a bath, only the usual tin tub, of course. I was pleased to learn recently that that hotel was still going strong, and not looking much different.

Next morning we set off in a hired car for Srinagar. As I look back, I feel some shame, as Quaker and I drove off in this comfortable car, while Daroga went in a crowded bus. That was a way of life. Probably, he preferred the company in the bus. I hope so.

The drive took the whole day, through the most spectacular country, first up a winding road out of the plains climbing to pine forests and cool air. Descending into the gorge of the river Jhelum, crossing over with the water below us, tumbling and roaring on its way to the plains. After we crossed the river the road ran for a long way beside it, curving in and out while it climbed to where the Vale of Kashmir spread out ahead. The violence all gone it flowed with more tranquillity. Here was Srinagar, a green valley with high mountains in the distance, wonderful after the dusty plains from which I had come.

I remembered that long ago my grandmother had made this journey to visit my uncle, stationed at Gilgit. She had travelled by bullock cart, taking several days on the journey, stopping at night at the little Dak bungalows (resthouses) I had seen and shot past in one day. The next time I visited Kashmir was about twenty-five years later, and we flew the whole way in a few hours. I believe this, my first visit, was much the best way. On arrival the car took me to the Bund, the last point to which cars could go. After that travel was all by water. A small boat, a *shikara*, took me across the river to the houseboats, belonging to my hostess.

There were three of these moored to the river bank, one behind the other, floating wooden homes, comfortable and attractive, with fantastic carving both inside and out, on the furniture and the boat itself. Always of flowers, fruit, foliage, or intricate designs. Never of people or animals as this was considered idolatrous, the carvers being strict Muslims. It was the same as regards the

Kashmir - Takht-e-Suleiman (Solomon's Throne) in background

embroidery that was to be seen everywhere, on curtains, cushions and covers, all done locally including carpets, or durries.

The three boats were connected by gangways, the first being for sitting and dining rooms, with a front hall-like space in the bow facing up river and open veranda-type above. There one could watch all the traffic of this great river floating past. Bedrooms, complete with their own bathrooms were in the next boat. Finally came that containing the kitchen and the servants' quarters.

It was an entertainment in itself to sit at one's ease, maybe with a cool drink at hand, gazing at the water-borne variety of boats passing by. Great barge-like vessels, doing the jobs of lorries on land, laden with goods of all kinds, from firewood to food. More common were the *shikaras*, long, narrow, little wooden skiffs with three men paddling aft. These, too, varied from plain working craft for everyday use to the ornately adorned for hire as taxis. These had deep mattresses for their passengers to sit on, with a roof from which hung curtains that could be drawn to give complete privacy, with embroidery on both curtains and mattress. Inside one could recline, floating to the destination of that day. Many a love affair must have been carried on in this romantic seclusion. Alas, my hostess was also my chaperone, always seeing I was in suitable company.

We went everywhere in *shikaras*, to the shops with names such as 'Suffering Moses' and 'Ganymede', made visits to the big Dal Lake, with the mountains as background, and to a moored boat in the middle from which we dived into the clear water. Other trips were to the Mughal gardens, the Shalimar among them, to walk peacefully with fountains playing. If any felt more energetic, there was the climb to the Takht-e-Suleiman, Solomon's Throne built on a 1000 ft mound from which was a superb view over Srinagar and the valley of Kashmir with waters of the river Jhelum making a shining path between Nedou's Hotel on one bank and the houseboats moored to the other. The shops with their carved tracery showed in the distance downstream. After the dry flat plains of Bihar, the mountains, river and the lake and all the flowering greenness was Paradise. Sadly as I now write it is all but impossible, certainly dangerous to visit this beautiful country in which I found such tranquillity.

9
And to Gulmarg
(when hotter and for a trek)

Soon even Srinagar was thought to be getting rather warm, there was an exodus of those on holiday to Gulmarg, a couple of thousand feet higher up. Again I was the paying guest of an Army widow, a dear old lady. Taking in what were really lodgers in the cool Hill resorts helped the British widows of Indian Army officers to eke out their paltry pensions. To have houseboats in Srinagar, a cottage in Gulmarg, or in places like Naini Tal or Mussoorie was very helpful both to their owners and to those not wanting to go to an hotel. This time my lodging was a small wooden house, with only one spare room, and had a very steep, sloping roof as the winter snow at that height was heavy, the slope was needed to prevent a deep layer forming.

To reach Gulmarg, it was possible to drive for a short way out of Srinagar. After that it became steep, with too many boulders and pine forests to make a road a reasonable proposition for an area only fully populated for part of the year. For the rest it was mainly buried under snow. Gulmarg is like a saucer sitting among the mountains, the lip on one side facing the valley of the river Jhelum, but the rest sloping into great heights. The saucer was like a great grassy meadow, and literally translated Gulmarg means Rose Meadow, a lovely name for an attractive place.

At Tangmarg everyone had to walk, or hire a pony, baggage was handed over to porters, stout hillmen able to carry up to 80lb loads up the hills. There was no other transport so I hired a pony by the month, a bright chestnut that I renamed Rufus. Thereafter Rufus and his owner reported for duty each morning, taking me on visits to friends, picnics in the forests or on the green slopes of the mountains. In the evenings I would ride to the Club in my long evening dress, with a shawl tied round my waist for decency's sake. Gulmarg was a Mecca for golfers with two top class courses and a Rabbit's course for beginners, so I did play a lot of golf.

As with so much of Kashmir the surroundings were magnificent, so pleasing to raise one's eyes to the hills, as in the Psalms, only these were mountains. I wanted to see much more of this glorious country, also I had got bored with rounds of golf, picnics, and spending the evening dancing to gramophone records at the Club. I had made friends with another girl, alone as I was, and she felt there should be more than this social round. We decided to go on a short trek. It is nothing nowadays for two girls to go off into the blue, but it was not the thing in 1934.

Gwen was a newcomer to India, though rather older than I; she was less experienced. I could speak Hindi at least, not a great help as Urdu or Kashmiri was spoken locally, but some use. I made the arrangements or '*bundobast*', hired a guide with his horse and some pack ponies for our baggage, and a mount for Daroga, the bearer without whom to have gone would have been unthinkable. Gwen and I each had our regular ponies. My hostess helped over food for our trip, and gave us her blessing, and off we set on what to us was an adventure.

During our first day, we travelled through forests gradually rising in height as we progressed, until we reached a Forest bungalow, a rest spot for Forest officers on tours of duty. We were warned to take flea powder, and used it liberally all over the *charpoys* (beds) before we put down our bedding. The original Forest officer who chose this spot for a bungalow had an eye for perfection. This was a perfect place, sited in a green glade, sloping down to give a wonderful view into the distance, with streams tumbling along their rocky beds on each side, the sound of the rushing water a lullaby in the night.

Dear Daroga was aching after an unaccustomed day in the saddle but still insisted on making up our beds, after we had given them the necessary treatment. There was a caretaker, the *chowkidar*, attached to the property who said he could provide us with a chicken curry, which was delicious. We had heard a flurry of chickens cackling shortly after he made his offer.

After a peaceful night we awoke to find a crowd waiting outside to see us, and learnt they had come expecting to receive medical treatment from us. When British government officers of all the services toured they always took a supply of simple medicines, and treated minor complaints as best they could. Therefore when the people around heard some sahibs were at the bungalow they expected to get the usual treatment. We let the side down badly; it had never occurred to me to take any medicines at all, even for ourselves, being young and healthy. Very bad management. All this had to be explained to our disbelieving audience, who left feeling most disappointed, some having come many miles, others in pain. It is hard to understand how word could have spread so far to so many in what appeared an unpopulated area. I felt dreadful, having let them down so badly, and lost so much face for the British Raj.

Gwen and I set off for a day out, leaving Daroga and the pack ponies behind, only our mounted guide going with us. As we climbed higher, there were fewer trees, and more boulders until even our sure-footed ponies were in difficulties and we continued on our own two feet. Reaching 11,000ft we climbed up the final slope and before us spread a vast flat green meadow. This was our objective. It seemed to stretch ahead for miles, a great grassy crater with mountains curving around, like a stadium for the Gods. After a rest, and our picnic lunch, Gwen and I could not resist a wild gallop on our gallant ponies on this arena. Well rested they seemed to enjoy this as much as we did. Our guide and his mount did not join us, he just stared at us shaking his head at our madness.

43

Soon he called us back, there was the descent to make, he was anxious to get back to the bungalow well before darkness fell. We were sad to leave this unspoilt and peaceful place, but happy to have been there. It was harder to climb down than up, with scree sliding under our feet, but we and our sturdy steeds slithered our way back, returning tired but full of satisfaction at having seen a glimpse of heaven. Daroga and the pack ponies had had a good rest. Another tasty curry was awaiting us and water had been heated so we could have a good wash. What more could we want.

After a leisurely start next morning we made for another Forest bungalow, rather an anti-climax, as we had expected to find it as delightfully sited as the first. Neither countryside nor bungalow were as fine as the one we had already visited, merely more hills and forests. We had seen the best. No crowd was waiting for attention the next morning, word had spread that we were useless. Now it was time to head for home, the major part of our journey taking us alongside a small stream and through more cultivated country.

Suddenly a group of men barred our way, and it was difficult to find out why. At last in a mixture of Kashmiri, Urdu and Hindi, I gathered that a bear had been causing great trouble in their village, and doing much damage and they wanted us to shoot it. I endeavoured to explain that we did not even have a gun with us. This they could not believe. All sahibs carried guns on tour. They eyed us closely, and then it dawned on them we were only girls in male attire, not the young sahibs as they had first thought. They shook their heads, said something in Kashmiri to our guide which was not translated.

As they turned away I asked on which side of the stream was the bear. 'The other' they said. So we stayed on the path this side. Once again we had let down the British Raj in not going to their help.

So back to the social life of Gulmarg. It had not been an arduous or tremendous trip, but we had enjoyed ourselves and seen a little of the natural beauty of this land of mountains, valleys and streams. Anyway neither of us could afford more than this modest effort.

10
Back to Patna
(21st Birthday Party - 1934)

In September, my father was given a fortnight's well-earned, and much-needed leave, so I left Gulmarg for Srinagar and the houseboat, to join him there. Knowing his love for fishing when he could get it I decided to arrange this. Taking the best advice I could get I booked a small Forest bungalow with a stream that had a good reputation for trout fishing. It was said to be an excellent stretch of water, the Middle Bringhi for those who know Kashmiri rivers.

Sadly my father had only been a few days in Srinagar, pleased at the prospect of the fishing to come, when a telegram came ordering him to attend a meeting in Patna, the provincial capital of Bihar. The Governor wished his presence to discuss the after-effects of the earthquake. It seemed grossly unfair to me after the stressful months he had been through and the long journey from Bihar to Kashmir, that he should have to leave so soon. However it was '*Hukum Hai*' or orders is orders.

Our fishing trip cancelled we set off for the long journey to Patna, first the day's drive to the plains, and nearly three more days in the train. It was not quite so hot as on my journey earlier in the year, but it was still uncomfortably warm, a more steamy heat being the end of the monsoon period.

The journey was not entirely without any incident. My dog, Quaker, no longer a tiny puppy, sat with me in the back of the car, my father sitting by the driver. I realised almost too late, that Quaker was about to be sick. I seized the nearest receptacle, and was just in time. Unluckily it was my father's favourite golfing cap, recently bought in Britain on his last leave. He was not pleased to have to consign it to the river Jhelum. Both dog and I knew we were in the doghouse for the rest of the day.

After arrival at Patna I saw little of my father; he was immersed in long meetings with the Governor and other senior men of the Province. He must have mentioned my photography during the earthquake as His Excellency asked to see the photos. I had not taken them with me to Kashmir, so I was invited to come and stay at Government House during the Patna Meet, due to take place soon, and to bring the photographs.

So a few weeks later I returned with my snaps for a most enjoyable visit. All 'Pomp and Ceremony' in front of His Excellency, the Governor and the public. Behind the scenes it was different. HE had a daughter, about my age, she, the *aides-de-camp*, plus myself and a young Police officer, a fellow guest like me, had a riotous time. It was made more fun since we had to behave ourselves so impeccably in the public view.

Tent-pegging at Patna Meet

One lasting memory is of the Police officer who had for some sin in our eyes been rolled up in a carpet, and had to be unrolled as hastily as possible when some dignitaries entered the room. I wonder if Spud remembers that, too.

Meanwhile back home I found that my father and the others had done an amazing job, while I had been away. I learnt that the whole factory floor had been turned round by 90 degrees, a complicated effort using the old machinery on new foundations. The earthquake had caused the old to sink in the incredible 'broth' that it had produced. The meeting with the Governor, in Patna which my father had attended was the first of many others all over the Province as HE toured the worst-hit areas of Bihar. Darbhanga District had been among those, especially Darbhanga town itself, turning it into piles of rubble. The Maharaja's two palaces had been damaged, the old Red Palace, Lalbagh, had had its tower collapse. All that was left standing of the White Palace was the lift shaft, a recent addition. The Maharaja, always anxious to entertain any VIP, decided Darbhanga should be the site for one of these meetings.

His White Palace was hastily restored, so his younger brother the Kumar Sahib was keen to do his share of entertainment. Hence one evening he gave a party for the visiting dignitaries and local gentlefolk, both British and Indian. As in all these big affairs all the food was imported from Calcutta. The guests wore evening dress, and everything was as elegant as possible, except for one thing.

The Kumar Sahib had a passion for dogs, not just any dog, but the celebrities of the dog world. He could not be called a true dog lover.

If he heard of a canine acquiring fame, he wanted that animal, among those he had collected was the hound in the old black and white film 'The Hound of the Baskervilles.' Champions abounded. The newest arrival went everywhere with him, becoming attached and adoring. Then a new prize came on the scene and the old favourite was despatched to the extensive kennels.

On this occasion the Kumar Sahib decided he would show off all his dogs; they were let loose among the guests. They had been living in kennels and were not house-trained; they became excited at this unusual outing. Soon a bevy of sweepers had to be sent for arriving with bottles of methylated spirit and floor cloths. Talk of going from the sublime to the ridiculous, the guests behaved impeccably even if the dogs did not. I've wondered since if the Kumar Sahib arranged this purposely as a joke, since he had a strange sense of humour, and could have got quite a kick out of the scene.

One of the actual meetings was held at the house of the manager, my godfather, Gerald, to discuss what was to be done in the aftermath of the earthquake, being the reason proper for the Governor's visit. At this a young *aide-de-camp* decided to relate a funny story he had heard about the lady who had been caught in her bath when the quake struck.

She had rushed out of the bathroom, dripping wet, clutching a small towel and calling out in Hindi '*Panch rupee dekhne waste*'. This means 'Five rupees for a look.' He had hoped to get a laugh. Instead there was a frozen silence for some moments. It was broken by the District Commissioner saying in a very frigid voice 'That was my wife'. After which everybody began talking loudly, while the ADC shrank down in his chair. The lady was the same one who had so appalled me when unable to talk to the Rani at Hathwa. Obviously she was trying to say five rupees not to look but her knowledge of Hindi had not improved greatly.

On 21 November that year I had my twenty-first birthday, and I had a party. It was no grand affair, no ballroom or dance band, it was a 'Scavenging Party'. For those who do not know what that is the competitors are given a list of items to collect. Ours was a trifle unusual as it included a live creature of some kind, the household pets were barred. Someone tried to get the turkey, there in preparation for Christmas, but failed. Some lizards were caught off the walls, but the prize went to the cane assistant who managed to ride onto the veranda on a buffalo.

Father in silver howdah during elephant procession at Darbhanga

11
Visits - 1935-1936
(from Viceroy and Governor)

As 1935 drew to a close big changes to my life were looming, my happiest years were round the corner. The first hint of this was in a letter from my uncle in Suffolk telling us that the son of great friends of his was coming out to Bihar to be assistant to the manager of the Maharaja of Darbhanga - incidentally my godfather, Gerald. Geoffrey duly arrived. I did just meet him but he was whisked off for basic training to the manager of one of the Maharaja's more distant estates. In the meantime, the Viceroy, Lord Willingdon had decided to pay a visit to north Bihar. The Maharaja was delighted at the prospect of more lavish entertaining. Lord and Lady Willingdon accepted his invitation. Geoffrey was brought back to Darbhanga to assist with all the preparations for this important occasion.

The Willingdons and their entourage were to stay in the Raj guest house. All the other guests, of whom there were many, were to be put up in a tented encampment on a large field nearby, complete with marquees as lounge and dining rooms. These were called *shamianas.*

Most of Geoffrey's duties then were to see that arrangements for the Viceregal party were perfect. After that he could attend to the other guests, among whom were my father and I, eating his meals with us. Noticing that Geoffrey would rush in at the last moment I always managed to keep a seat beside me vacant, strangely Geoffrey always made for it.

The chief entertainment was an evening party held in Lalbagh, the Red Palace that backed on to a lake, the windows overlooking the water. From a houseboat on the lake was set off a dazzling display of fireworks. In the background were set pieces presented from the far bank. The glamorous setting with its brilliant reflections from the water made a wonderful spectacle, as we watched from the palace windows. It was the most romantic moment for me, as I stood there, with a handsome young man beside me. Geoffrey should have been attending to his other duties, but found some time to spend with me, and to dance with me later on.

Once the fireworks were over a band imported from Calcutta took over and we danced in exotic surroundings, the floor was of brightly coloured mosaic, unfortunately very hard on the feet. Like Eliza Doolittle I 'could have danced all night' in spite of that. Against the highly-coloured walls stood carved ivory chairs, said to have belonged to Warren Hastings. Some may remember he was impeached for taking possession of too much, amongst other things. However, he does seem to have left these chairs, and the carved ivory elephant *howdah* I have mentioned earlier.

49

In the centre of all this stood the Maharaja, resplendent in a gold-coloured brocade coat, strung across his turban was Marie Antoinette's famous diamond necklace, topped by a white egret's feather held in place by a pear-shaped pearl brooch. The sparkling jewels vying with the fireworks in their brilliance, quite outshone Lord and Lady Willingdon. The whole evening could have come from Hollywood's most romantic film. Next day the party was over and everyone went back to their normal lives, an anti-climax.

Luckily for me my father decided we should show hospitality to this young man, about whom my uncle had written to us. We asked Geoffrey to visit us at the weekend. When my father found Geoffrey was a good sort and keen to go duck shooting with him, he was asked out for every weekend he could manage. The season had only just begun, and Geoffrey got away frequently. Normally I am not at all keen on early rising, but found myself getting up at 4am to accompany the pair of them to catch the dawn flight. Something I had not imagined I could want to do. As things turned out I did a lot of this kind of thing over future years, paddling through muddy pools in the half light. Or keeping still and silent crouched in a ditch fighting off cramp in order to mark fallen birds, and actually doing it willingly.

Father and Geoffrey relaxing on the verandah, 1936

Geoffrey did try to kiss me on one of these weekend visits but I turned away. I knew that he meant more to me than a casual kiss, and wanted no part in what could become a frivolous affair I had indulged in before. Things might have stayed like this had not the Maharaja embarked on more entertaining. This time it was for a newly-appointed Governor of the Province, who was touring it after his inauguration.

Although not nearly so momentous an affair as the Viceroy's visit, preparations had been made and all was ready for His Excellency's arrival in January 1936. Then came the news of the death of King George V, Court mourning putting a stop to all official entertainment. The visit was cancelled.

Since the caterers were there, and food prepared, the Maharaja decided it should not be wasted. Nearby friends, my father and I included, were invited to a private dinner party. After it I was asked if I had seen the photographs of the Viceroy's visit, happily for me I had not, but would like to see them. Geoffrey was told to take me up to the Private Office on the floor above. So there we were seated on a couch, turning over the pages of a photograph album, full of photos of ourselves among the many others.

Details can be imagined, but the outcome was that I was in Geoffrey's arms and he was asking me to marry him. I did not refuse him this time. When we realised we must join the others I saw to my horror, his black dinner jacket was now speckled with white fur all over the front. I had been wearing my white fur cape, since January, even on the plains of India, can be chilly in the evening.

There was nothing he could do about this except to face the rest of the party. Nothing was said at our entrance except that I thanked His Highness. The guests all left making no comments, some including ourselves were staying overnight. Among these was the Raja of Mayurbhanj, a petty princeling, anxious to shoot crocodile. An arrangement had already been made for early next morning.

Since all was prepared, the *bundobast* made, it was decided to carry on, with Geoffrey in charge of the expedition. My father agreed to join the group, and, since Geoffrey was going, I wanted to go, too.

We set off on elephants to make for the river that was home to the crocodiles we were after. There are two kinds, the narrow-nosed *garial*, a fish eater and the broad-nosed *mugger*. The latter will lie in wait for women coming to the river to fill their pots with water, and attack. I was told of one, who when killed and opened up, had a belly full of bangles, and anklets. We were after a *mugger*.

Using elephants our advance did not disturb other animals as we made our way through elephant grass, growing tall enough to hide an eleven foot high elephant. Sitting on mattress-like pads, tied across the great beasts' backs, we clutched at the straps to keep our balance against the rolling gait. I preferred not to watch what happened when our target was reached, but know of the procedure.

It was customary to have men ready and waiting with inflated animal bladders tied by lengths of light rope to spears. As soon as a croc was shot they threw their spears. Crocodiles dive immediately when in trouble down into the depths of the muddied water. It is then impossible to locate them or know if dead, wounded, or still alive. The bladders act as floats and show their position. If dead or wounded they can be hauled to the surface. If alive they easily escape.

Certainly the guest of honour looked pleased with himself, but I had got my *mahout* to keep in the background. I was only there for the ride and because of Geoffrey's presence. Next day my father and I returned home, no mention was made by either of us of Geoffrey. The following weekend he visited us, and formally asked my father's permission to marry me. I think my father was thankful to give it, as Geoffrey was just the kind of son-in-law he must have hoped for; they always got on so well together. There was no hope of an early wedding; Geoffrey was only newly joined and poorly paid and living in a room in the Raj guest house. The Maharaja, in spite of his great wealth, was not renowned for paying high salaries, only slightly less mean than his late father.

That gentleman when asked by one of his managers for a rise in pay was told he ought to be sacked if he was such a fool as not to have made enough on the side. That had been the attitude, now it was somewhat better. All the same we had no idea how long we would have to wait, Geoffrey being an honest man, and not given to taking backhanders.

12
Marriage - 1937
(honeymoon in Cawnpore)

Illness dogged our lives over the next few months. While playing tennis I collapsed with acute appendicitis and was rushed to the Civil Hospital; the only one there was in a large district. Serving mainly the local population it had three single rooms for what we now call 'private patients'. Luckily we were a healthy crowd on the whole, so there was no waiting list.

Three British nursing sisters, Biddy, Joey and Zeissy, cared for the whole hospital and did sterling work for Indians and Europeans alike, with Indian nurses to help. A British Civil Surgeon, a Colonel in the Indian Medical Service, was in charge with Indian doctors under him. I regret to say I have a very low opinion of the Colonel but he did succeed in operating on my appendix eventually. His first incision was too high up, so he continued to cut on downwards, resulting in a ten inch scar to remember him by. I was kept in hospital for over two weeks, which pleased me since Geoffrey's HQ was only a couple of miles away and he was able to visit me daily.

Then the Maharaja decided that his silverware and other valuables needed professional attention only available in Calcutta. Knowing Geoffrey could be trusted with his treasures the Maharaja ordered him to see they got safely to Hamilton's, well-known jewellers of Calcutta.

While delivering all these items of great price, Geoffrey mentioned he was looking for an engagement ring. The firm was grateful to the man who had brought them this large order, and the very beautiful ring I was given did not cost as much as it might have done.

Geoffrey was the next to be struck down, and quite unnecessarily I am convinced. There was a tennis club at the Civil HQ near Darbhanga town and the hospital, where all who could would play. Geoffrey was there one day with his Sealyham and one of the nurses, Biddy, had brought her small terrier. These two dogs hated each other and got into a fight. In separating them Geoffrey got bitten; Biddy took him off to the hospital, and saw that he had all the treatment needed. Next morning Geoffrey turned up at his boss' office with a bandaged hand. Gerald, his boss, wanted to know what had happened and was told. As soon as the words 'dog bite' were mentioned Gerald over-reacted; Geoffrey must have anti-rabies injections. This was not a simple matter then for there were not many places in India which held a supply of the vaccine. The nearest was Patna, a twenty-four hour journey away by train. A *chaprassi*, an orderly, was sent off armed with a thermos flask to collect the serum. It was nearly three days before he returned with it.

It is a fact that a rabid dog would have shown obvious symptoms by then, but both dogs behaved normally. The Civil Surgeon went to see Gerald.

'Neither dog has rabies, so there is no need for any injections,' he said.

'Geoffrey is my responsibility,' replied Gerald. 'I insist he has them.'

After a week of large injections in Geoffrey's stomach, the doctor spoke to Gerald again.

'Both dogs are still alive and well so there is absolutely no need for any further treatment. They would be dead by now if rabid.'

Gerald would not listen. 'I am not taking any chances; Geoffrey must finish the course.'

Geoffrey and the doctor had to give in as autocratic Gerald had to be obeyed, and a further seven of these horrible jabs went into an already painful stomach. A few days later Geoffrey found that when he tried to get out of bed his knees gave way under him. He could not use his hands to hold anything. From the elbows down his arms were paralysed - an appalling experience.

He sent a message by word of mouth to Gerald, who then sent a car to let my father and me know what happened. We hurried in; my father was furious with Gerald, blaming him entirely. Telegrams were sent to the Pasteur Institute in Simla, the only people who knew anything about rabies and its treatment. They wired back that this did happen in one in ten thousand cases and they knew no remedy. This was terrifying information.

We did not know what to do and it was a dreadful time with the prospect of Geoffrey permanently paralysed at the age of twenty-three.

As it happened my father was due home leave soon and, much against my will, I was to go with him. Realising he must do something helpful, Gerald arranged for Geoffrey to travel to Britain with us. I was delighted.

This meant the usual train journey to Calcutta overnight and the much longer one to Bombay. As I have said before, Indian trains are high off the ground with awkward steps up to the carriages. Geoffrey could not climb up so my father had to stand in the carriage doorway and pull while Daroga, our stalwart bearer, with hands on Geoffrey's bottom, pushed him up. I was not much help as I was recovering from my recent drastic appendix operation. My poor father had to sleep on the top bunk while us two youngsters had the bottom berths. Reaching Bombay, we found that P & O had laid on a wheel chair to get Geoffrey on board, but he was appalled at the idea and insisted on shuffling up the gangway. Life was easier on board, with lifts and very helpful stewards to dress and shave him.

In London Geoffrey's mother was there to greet him; a dazzling person with whom I always got on well. I never had any mother-in-law trouble. She had arranged for Geoffrey to have massage treatment and gradually he responded to this, to the joy of us all.

By the time my father's leave ended Geoffrey was fit enough to return to India with us. This was a very happy voyage and helped to complete his recovery.

Just engaged (note arm-band to mark death of George V; and the two dogs, Susie and Quaker)

I had received much teasing from my uncle when I had arrived in England engaged to Geoffrey. He told me he had not meant me to go this far when he had written asking me to be friendly to this young man. All the same, he and my aunt were delighted and I was approved of by the various future in-laws. A daunting experience, the most awesome of which was a lunch at Fortnum's submitting to examination by two of Geoffrey's aunts.

When considering what had happened to Geoffrey and what had caused this, it is just possible that the Pasteur Institute was right. He may have been allergic to the serum. Personally I do not believe this. Consider how that serum travelled for a night in a thermos flask in the care of an uneducated man. How many times was it opened en route to show his fellow travellers? Did it retain the correct temperature? Another possibility is that Geoffrey did far too much while having the injections. Years later when I had to have these anti-rabies jabs I was told not to take exercise. Geoffrey had to carry on his duties at the various palaces by cycle, which certainly means using hands and legs, covering quite a distance. However we did not entirely ignore the Pasteur Institute's advice to keep clear of any more anti-rabic treatment, but still kept our much loved dogs.

Think what would happen if something like this occurred nowadays - there would be demands for large sums in compensation from employers. The Maharaja could have afforded to pay, though he would have fought for every pice. In those days we accepted that something had gone wrong but did not blame anyone.

While I was in England I took the opportunity of gathering up a *trousseau*, not knowing when we would be able to get married. I even had a wedding dress made, in beautiful ripple satin, costing what was, to me, the huge sum of seven pounds and ten shillings; the most expensive garment I had ever had. That was in 1936. I would be surprised if I could get such a lovely gown for seven hundred pounds today, over fifty years later. For friends and relations though this was a great chance to hand over wedding presents instead of having to post them to India when the day dawned. So I returned to India complete with wedding dress, *trousseau* and presents but with no idea when we could get married.

Depressing events had been happening while we were away, which did eventually hasten that happy day for us.

The manager of Pandaul, the Maharaja's estate of which my father had been manager when I was born, had taken to drink. He had always been a great party person but now it was not only at parties that he drank too much. He had become much worse since the earthquake, during which he had had a narrow escape. He had reached a point where he was in a state of the DTs for most of the time.

His wife, Jess, a most charming American, tried hard to prevent any alcohol getting to him but there was always someone in the bazaar who would supply it. This meant the liquor he got was not quality but a poisonous brew. The

General Manager, Gerald, sent him several warnings but Paddy had gone beyond noticing and eventually was given the sack. He and Jess went to stay with friends nearby and Geoffrey was made manager. It was an awkward situation for me; these were good friends of mine and they were very resentful. All the same, Geoffrey being given this post brought our marriage nearer.

In spite of his wife and friends, Paddy succeeded in getting an excess of alcohol of poor quality and within a month had drunk himself to death. The Christian graveyard was on Pandaul estate land and one of Geoffrey's first tasks was, on hearing of Paddy's death, to spend most of the night digging a grave by lantern light. Paddy was buried next morning near to the grave where lay my mother. Time could never be long between death and the funeral in India in those days. Geoffrey was distressed but now he had both a bungalow and a better job.

Strangely enough, during almost twenty years between my father being manager at Pandaul and Geoffrey taking over the post, every single manager had died of drink and was buried there. Hopefully now this horrid spell was broken.

Geoffrey was now only six miles away from us at the sugar factory and I used to ride over every morning and have breakfast with him, riding back afterwards. Most evenings Geoffrey would ride over and have dinner with us; riding back by moonlight afterwards, so we saw plenty of each other.

Plans for our wedding could now be made - when we heard that Bishop Foss Westcott, Metropolitan of India, from Calcutta was coming to Bihar on tour the following February, it seemed perfect. We wrote asking if he would perform our wedding ceremony on February 14 - Valentine's Day. He agreed to preside but it had to be 17 February 1937, to which proposal we agreed happily.

The Maharaja offered the Raj Guest House to be used as the church, as there was none for seventy odd miles. This was ideal as it had a long drawing room with big windows along both sides and an alcove at the end. Gerald and Helen, his wife, offered their house and garden for the reception. However I was the one who had to arrange everything else, both locally and from Calcutta - even the bouquets!

The Calcutta caterers were well used to coming to Darbhanga for the many functions; this was small in comparison. Everything began to fit in wonderfully, including the fact that Geoffrey's parents were both to be in Cawnpore, although they lived in Sussex.

The great day dawned - the Raj Guest House looked just right with flowers arranged in each window. I was able to sweep down the aisle on my father's arm, with Geoffrey awaiting me in the alcove; a table as an altar.

On coming out we were greeted by the Maharaja's mounted bodyguard, who lined the way to the reception, pennants flying from their lances, giving extra glamour to a glorious day; the first of many spent during our fifty-one years together.

There was one hitch - only a small one. We were spending our honeymoon in Cawnpore at the home of Geoffrey's parents, who had vacated it for our first

At the wedding reception, Darbhanga

58

week. This meant the usual night's train journey needed to get anywhere distant-
so often the way in India. Among our wedding presents was a handsome picnic
box. Geoffrey's mother offered to have this filled with some supper for our
journey. This she very kindly did and locked it.... but forgot to give us the key.

We did not want to spoil our super present and, anyway, had no tools with
which to break it open. We were both hungry, not having eaten much beyond a
slice of cake. At the first biggish station we were able to buy a loaf, a tin of butter
and one of asparagus, which the staff kindly opened for us and buttered slices of
bread. This was our supper and it tasted delicious. From that day on, whenever
we could we would have asparagus with bread and butter on our wedding
anniversaries.

In my bedding roll I found a bottle of champagne which my father's
khansamah, or butler, had obviously filched at the reception. A great gesture,
especially since he was a Muslim, and much appreciated by us.

Next morning we got to Lucknow, where we were to change trains. With
some hours to spend, we visited the Residency: the place where the British put
up such a magnificent defence during the Mutiny in 1857. Then on to Cawnpore,
driving out to Lake House, the lovely place where we spent our honeymoon.

Geoffrey on steps of Lake House, Cawnpore, on honeymoon

59

Lake House later became part of an area known as Allenbagh, a reserve. It was on what was almost an island joined to the mainland only by a narrow causeway, the brainchild of uncle George Allen.

Geoffrey's grandfather had been in India since Mutiny days, starting up the 'Civil and Military Gazette' in Allahabad. It was he who actually took the young Rudyard Kipling with him on the ship out to India to work on his newspaper. This gave Kipling his start as a writer. When grandfather, Sir George Allen, left India for a life in Sussex his eldest son, another George, remained and became a very wealthy man but also benevolent.

Around Cawnpore was an area of arid ravines, craggy hillocks covered with boulders down to the dusty valleys, but not far from the river Ganges. Uncle George saw the possibilities; he approached the Government, then British, with his idea. This was to run off some of the water from the Ganges and lead it into the dry gullies. The Government agreed, if he did it at his own expense - which he did. Diverting this water made the area green and wooded. Little islands were formed between the stretches of water. With the greenery came animals: birds nested in the trees that soon grew and wild ducks swam and flew along the waterways. The Government allowed Uncle George to build a house at one end which was the flattest. He called it 'The Retreat'. He built a summerhouse at the far end which became Lake House. These buildings were left to Geoffrey's father on his eldest brother's death. He and my mother-in-law entertained Queen Mary there when she and King George V visited India for the Delhi Durbar in 1911. The poor lady was laid low with tummy trouble; not wanting publicity she stayed with them at 'The Retreat' to recover in peace and quiet. My eldest son now has the Visitor's Book with her signature as a guest.

My father-in-law was not the businessman his brother had been; difficult times forced him to sell the property. The Indian Government permitted the Allen family to keep the right to use Lake House as long as an Allen lived in India. That ended when we left the country in 1970, ending about 120 years of Allens in India.

Two wings, with a bathroom and bedroom were added to the original structure and Mr and Mrs Charles Allen, Geoffrey's parents, sometimes lived in it. It was there we went, spending much of our time paddling in the small boat they had up and down these channels of water, having picnics in green glades on the islands and watching all the wild life that now abounded.

We had no great wish to spend much time in Cawnpore city itself and it had become difficult to be away for long. We had felt we must take Geoffrey's little Sealyham, Susie, with us. Geoffrey had spent the Christmas before, camping not far outside my father's garden. This was territory under his charge in which he could be officially on tour. Susie had come in heat and a servant on guard was left in the tent with her while Geoffrey joined us for the Christmas festivities.

I kept an eye on Quaker, my spaniel, but as our guests were leaving he disappeared. As soon as this was realised Geoffrey rushed to his tent but was too late - the servant was fast asleep and Quaker and Susie had celebrated Christmas their way.

Since Susie was small, eight years old and had never had pups before, we were worried about her. Quaker was a big dog. We realised that the pups were due during our honeymoon so she came too. As Cawnpore had a real vet she was given a proper examination and we were told there would not be more than two puppies. We stayed within reach until one evening, when we were invited out to a party we could not refuse. Of course that was the evening Susie chose, perhaps wisely not wanting a fuss. We came home to a beaming bearer, happy to inform us that there was one puppy. That was all she had. We called him Toby, as he looked like Punch's dog Toby, and decided he was a wedding present from Quaker and Susie - all they could give us - and one we loved very much.

13
Life at Pandaul
(pig-sticking and malaria)

Our honeymoon over, we returned to Pandaul to start a new life where I had been born. Now Geoffrey was the manager of the Estate as my father had been. The old bungalow had come down in the earthquake and a smaller brick one had been built just in front of the old site. We wondered how this would affect the ghost who was reputed to be that of a *sahib* who drove a pony and trap up the front steps of the old building - now this spot was our back veranda. Certainly we never heard the distinct sound of carriage wheels swishing to a stop, as we had been told used to occur.

The new house was neither as cool or as roomy as the old one, without electricity, so no light or fans. We did have a refrigerator run on kerosene, a luxury my mother had not had. Cheques given to us as wedding presents had been spent on this. We were back to oil lamps and hand-pulled *punkahs*.

The bungalow at Pandaul

Changes in housekeeping came to my notice; chickens for cooking were graded at three rates: roasting, boiling or soup. At my father's these were charged at six, five and four annas respectively, an anna being worth a penny farthing in the money of those days. Now I only had to pay five, four and three annas each. On enquiring about this, I was told that my husband was only a '*Chota Sahib*'-

a junior - so the price was less. The '*Burra Sahibs*' - the seniors - were expected to pay more. All very reasonable I thought.

Everyone seemed determined I should know my place. When, with great pride, I showed my father's old bearer, Daroga, my beautiful wedding presents he agreed they were very fine. However, he then went on to point out that I now lived in a very small bungalow. He was not going to have me trying to outdo my father. To keep one's proper place is important in India. Geoffrey was now one of the suppliers of sugar cane to the factory of which my father was manager.

It was early March when we returned from our honeymoon and before long what were known as the Kurrian winds, which were roasting, would begin to blow, drying up all greenness - a signal for the threshing of many crops to begin. Little sugar cane was still standing in the fields but there was one very thick patch not yet cut. When the labourers began work on this they gave up, telling Geoffrey there was an aggressive wild boar living there which was threatening them.

These were the days when pig-sticking was a recognised sport, with the Kadir Cup competed for by all keen pig-sticking champions. Tastes in the shape of the spear's blade were compared, my husband and father differing in their choice. Local pig-sticks were arranged when conditions were right; this was the right moment. Geoffrey sent information round the district that there would be such an event.

My father and two others from the factory came; more from the surrounding area, even the Superintendent of Police from the District Headquarters twenty-five miles away turned up, the horses being sent ahead. All were mounted complete with their particular spear and I, too, got ready to ride my Cavalier but there was an outcry from both husband and father, backed by the others. I was ordered to give up the idea. I never intended carrying a spear, just wanting to go along 'for the ride'. Instead I was told I could have Hira Prasad, a young elephant, perhaps only a teenager, as my mount. They say elephants never forget - perhaps he has not remembered me but I will not forget him.

Beating began to flush out; the boar men with sticks hitting at tins and yelling, trying to stampede the boar onto the far side. There the riders, spears at the ready, lined up to give chase the moment their quarry appeared. Nothing happened.

The beaters complained that the cane was too thick to penetrate. Geoffrey, fearing a fiasco, conferred with my father. Together they agreed that if Geoffrey used his newly-acquired tractor to attack the cane my father would see that the mangled cane would be accepted for milling. This plan went into action and the tractor was sent in to demolish the boar's hideout, but things took an unexpected turn.

Instead of being driven out towards the horsemen, the old boar darted past the tractor, coming out just by where I, on my elephant, had been positioned to keep me out of the way. Hira Prasad got wildly excited and took off after it, trunk up in air and tail waving. The *mahout* encouraged him, I encouraged the mahout and we led the field.

The boar headed for a nearby village, with the narrowest of paths running between the houses. Hira Prasad followed at a gallop. There was no room for the riders to pass us until we had cleared the houses and were out in the open fields. The riders then charged past and we were left behind. Having no wish to see the outcome of the chase after my moment of glory, that was enough.

I do not remember who got 'first spear' in triumph, but the curved tusks were mounted on a stand and a small gong hung below, which was given to us. Pig-sticking was then traditional and acceptable and I did accept it, but could not bring myself to watch the gory finale. It was a very dangerous sport, over open country, the boar sometimes turning and charging. Horses were brought down and their riders killed. I imagine the beaters got a good pork addition to their rice, being neither Muslims nor high caste Hindus. I told the *mahout* to make for home and he and Hira Prasad did so, to oblige me. Most days did not hold such excitement.

It was not long after this event that I realised I was pregnant. The local population seemed to know almost as soon as I did, which was a surprise until one thought about it. Remember we only had 'thunderboxes' for sanitation. It was the sweeper's job to empty these so he had the most intimate knowledge of the workings of one's bodily functions.

One morning a deputation, headed by the village schoolmaster, came to the bungalow asking to see me. I was presented with a bunch of bananas and told that it was their custom to give a present of food to a woman newly with child. They hoped I would accept and eat these bananas; this I said I would be happy to do.

I did wonder if perhaps the village felt some responsibility for my pregnancy since soon after our return from our honeymoon it was the time of the Hindu Spring Festival. During the ceremonies the *pujari* - the priest - had come to us and placed green shoots on our heads, praying as he sprinkled us with a pink liquid, generally used very liberally by everyone on all and sundry during this festival of 'Holi'. Most non-Hindus kept themselves out of the way on this day but in our position it would have been rude. No doubt the *pujari* was delighted since the rites of Holi were for fertility. We had not planned for offspring so soon but who can stand against such potent symbols?

The villagers rejoiced for, not only had every manager since my father left died of drink, but none of them had had a child. I was the last baby to have been born to one of the managers, twenty-three years earlier.

Sadly the general rejoicing was cut short by the terrible epidemic that struck locally. Virulent malaria hit Pandaul village and its environs; it was so bad and the people were so sick that the Maharaja sent them food: rice, lentils and vegetables. Then it was found that too few were strong enough to cook for all the rest and kitchens had to be set up centrally. Although it was not a big place there were over 500 deaths in the village itself, and many more in the surrounding areas.

Even with regular dosing with quinine, the only anti-malaria medicine, Geoffrey spent about a week in each month with the typical very high temperature, shivering, aches and vomiting with which malaria hits. These periodic attacks continued for some months. All our servants were laid low. I became a good nurse for malarial patients and yet never had malaria myself. I did not take any medicines, being fearful that quinine might harm my unborn baby.

That baby was my son Michael and the strange thing is that he has never had malaria either, in spite of having served during all of his Army career in so many countries in the East. My other two children, born elsewhere in India did get malaria, though they did not spend long out of Britain.

During periods when Geoffrey was fit enough he would rally squads of *Doms* from outside our district. So low in the Hindu caste system were they that they could and would handle dead bodies. Our villagers were so weak they were throwing corpses into the nearby water source instead of burning them on funeral pyres in the customary Hindu way. The water source was a 'tank', a man-made lake, dug as famine relief work; the starving being given food for their labour; and providing an amenity, as the monsoon rains could then be conserved. It was into these 'tanks' that the dead were thrown. With the help of the *Doms* my husband got the bodies dragged out and burnt with the aid of gallons of kerosene oil. Not a pleasant task but it was only due to his actions that cholera did not follow and wipe out the survivors.

An expert came eventually from Calcutta, Professor Ramsey of the Ross Institute, and gave advice for prevention. Spraying with DDT and the draining of waterlogged areas where the anopheles mosquitoes, the carrier of malaria bred, helped to prevent such an epidemic occurring again. I have recently corresponded with the Ross Institute in London who were interested and asked for more details but were unable to account for Michael's and my immunity.

Another unpleasant event occurred about then. One of the bullocks, used for ploughing and drawing the main vehicle, the bullock cart, was bitten on the nose by a rabid jackal. Pandaul Estate belonged to the Maharaja, not only a Hindu but a high caste Brahmin, to whom the cow is sacred. On no account may they be killed so this poor animal could not be destroyed. Since rabies is contagious if the saliva of a rabid animal gets into the bloodstream through a wound or even a graze, it is necessary not to let this happen. There was then anyway no known way of recovering; death was inevitable, so the suffering creature was corralled until it died. Luckily nothing lives long when rabid. Although the pen was across the river from our bungalow we could hear its pitiful bellowing night and day during the few days it survived. Geoffrey could do nothing. If he had shot it he might well have been attacked.

14
Raising a Family
(1938-1940)

As I was now married, settled and with a grandchild on the way for him, my father, whose retirement was due, decided he would remain in India. There seemed no point in going to England, a much less familiar country to him, with his loved ones in India. He and his devoted bearer, Daroga, departed for Shillong, a hill station in Assam on the eastern border of India, not so well known nor so high as Simla or Darjeeling. It was unknown territory to him but proved an ideal location, all our family have since spent many happy hours there.

After a sixty-three mile long drive from the railhead in the plains, first through paddy fields and then more tropical jungle until the road passes through pine forest into a saucer-like valley, with pine woods dotting it, he moved into an hotel called the Pinewood Hotel, run by a delightful Swiss couple. Monsieur and Madame gave all a great welcome there. There was an excellent golf course, of which my father eventually became Secretary and even a small race course; the horses being small hill ponies with local jockeys.

The surrounding hill country was beautiful with good roads leading to delightful walks and picnic spots with small waterfalls cascading into glens of purple rhododendrons. Not far off was Cherrapunji, said to hold the world record for the most rainfall. Over the years we went there often and it certainly did not rain on each visit. Many years earlier British soldiers had been stationed there and the rate of suicides was so high they were withdrawn. It is said they threw themselves over the steep precipice from the plateau that forms Cherrapunji itself and gives a wonderful view over the plains of Assam. From there drops a waterfall that is spectacular in its height.

When the hot weather was well upon the plains my father invited me to visit him in Shillong. What with the heat and my pregnancy, Geoffrey thought this an excellent idea for me to escape for a short break. It certainly was a pleasant change to have a few weeks in the cool and in such lovely surroundings; this was the first of many stays in Shillong.

When the cold weather began my father joined us at Pandaul, and it was just as well that he did. I began having pains very early on the morning of Monday 10 January 1938. Geoffrey asked the local Dr Babu, not a well-qualified medico, but our only one, to see me. He came, but felt it impolite to touch me. He and my new *ayah* had a consultation and decided these were false pains, sometimes occurring a fortnight or so before giving birth. I thought they must be right. *Ayah*, who had recently come to me from friends whose children had gone to school in England had had a large family of her own. Also it was earlier than I had expected. I carried on thinking that if these were false pains what would the real ones be like!

At lunch I made an appearance and tried to eat, saying nothing to anybody, then retired to my bed. When I did not appear for tea my father came to see why. He took one look at me in obvious pain and took charge; Geoffrey was sent for; *ayah* was ordered to pack for me and we were pushed into the car almost forcibly. I still had twenty-five miles of bad road between me and the hospital.

It was nearly 8pm when we got there; not really very late. The Civil Surgeon was sent for and arrived grumbling that he had hoped for an early night as he had been out duck shooting all the previous day. Michael was born by 10pm, not too late, because I had been cut to hurry things up and given six stitches. Later I realised what a big mistake we'd made.

Instead of calling in Dr Babu, who never dealt with women, we should have called upon the services of the village *dai*, the midwife, vastly more experienced. However this was not considered quite the right thing. I should have let her deliver the baby, but I have to admit she did not have much idea of hygiene so perhaps it was better for baby and me to be in the good hands of my nurse friends at the hospital.

I spent two weeks in hospital, not even allowed out of bed for the first week - this was normal procedure then. I was glad to have the time to look after my new baby as I had never, ever even touched a baby before in my whole life.

On our return to Pandaul the village showed its delight; the local band, known to us as the Phoo-phoo band, were at the gate to greet us and escorted us up the long drive between the two lines of casuarina trees, to the bungalow steps. There we had to exhibit our son as the villagers filed past to see him. The band went on playing..... and went on playing. Since neither Michael nor I could get to sleep we had to ask them to stop. Luckily Michael was a tough boy to survive my ignorance, and with no clinics at hand to advise.

My dog, Quaker the spaniel, took Mike under his care. Previously when with Geoffrey and me out riding, Quaker would comb every cane brake and investigate each clump of bushes; now he accompanied *ayah* and the pram, keeping alongside all the time. No wandering off when on duty! As Mike began toddling he developed a tendency, when in the garden, to make for the flower beds and pick up manure, which went straight into his mouth. With Quaker's help we were able to relax on the lawn in our easy chairs and let Mike go free, or almost free, because we tied his baby reins to Quaker's lead. Off they would go together and when the inviting manure got too close we would call Quaker. Very gently the dog would turn and come back to us and the child had to come as well. Now we could sit in the garden in the cool of the evening without having to leap up all the time to retrieve our son.

Funnily enough Mike is the keen gardener of the family and still thinks manure is very good stuff. He will go out of his way to get hold of some - for his garden of course!

Conveniently for us Bishop Foss Westcott was due to do his annual tour to Bihar to visit us and was happy to christen Mike, accompanied as when he performed our marriage ceremony, by the north Bihar Chaplain, the Reverend Ethelred Judah.

One layer of our wedding cake had been taken off and soldered up into a tin by the Chief Engineer at the factory, to protect it against the weather and things such as weevils. On opening it up, the cake itself was found to be in excellent condition but the icing had melted. Heat of soldering or weather - who knows? A fresh coat of icing turned it into a beautiful christening cake.

The rest of 1938 passed peacefully; we were not aware in our rural retreat of the rumblings of war. My father spent the summer in the cool of the hills. Geoffrey was able to get a fortnight's local leave and we were able to join my father at his comfortable hotel. Madame was helpful with baby Mike and confided to me that she and Monsieur had so wanted a baby. 'We have tried and tried,' she said, 'but it is no use', and gave a great shrug of her shoulders. In the cold weather my father rejoined us. This was a pleasant arrangement, suiting us all, and he was there for Mike's first birthday.

The next excitement came a few months later when some villagers came asking for Geoffrey's help in ridding them of a troublesome crocodile, which was attacking the women when they went to collect water from the river. Returning from a successful expedition with his trophy, Geoffrey proudly displayed it before his son. Mike was only about eighteen months old and gave it one horrified look, then shrieked, much to his father's disappointment. I felt much the same as my son, especially as I was feeling queasy myself owing to my second baby being on the way.

Later this crocodile skin was made into the seat of a long, low stool which, when tipped a little made a wonderful slide for small children. Some years of being slid upon gave it a most wonderful polish. It became one of our most loved possessions, very coveted but, when dividing up my household goods and pieces on Geoffrey's death, I decided Mike should have it - he had seen it first, even if he did not like it then.

My father had got into a routine of spending his winters with us and the summers in the Shillong hotel. In mid-August 1939 he invited young Mike and me for a break in the cool. With number two on the way it was a relief to get out of the heat. Rumours of war could not be escaped; boiling up into reality on 3 September as many will remember.

Geoffrey immediately volunteered for the Forces. The Maharaja was very angry at this, telling him it was quite unnecessary as he, the Maharaja, could have prevented his call-up. Geoffrey refused to consider his suggestion, whereupon he was given orders to move to another estate; not at all convenient with the new baby due shortly.

The previous manager, being a Captain in the Bihar Light Horse, had been called up at once. Geoffrey was only a trooper. It was a more senior posting;

perhaps the Maharaja thought Geoffrey might be more willing to carry on; I admit I hoped he would, but he was not.

We moved in early November 1939 and at least the weather was pleasant but, at seven months' pregnant, it was very tiresome. A double horse box was loaded up with one cat, two horses, three dogs, four rabbits and five white fantail pigeons. Two *syces* (grooms) travelled with them; an overnight train journey to our new posting.

At Pandaul I had been on my home ground with friends nearby and a hospital with which I was familiar. Now I knew no-one and had no near neighbours and no hospital for miles. There was a big lake a few hundred yards in front of the bungalow and I was terrified the not-yet-two year old Mike would drown himself in it, as it was deep. Geoffrey would go spear fishing at night in a small boat with a torch to attract the fish. One night he saw two eyes gleaming in the torchlight; he aimed his spear at them; there was a tussle and much splashing and turmoil at the end of which he found he had speared a young crocodile. This did become an elegant little writing case. This also made me more alarmed that it was not only drowning facing Mike but being taken by a crocodile. Luckily for me, Geoffrey's father was paying one of his visits to India and was living at Lake House, Cawnpore, where we had spent our honeymoon. Geoffrey was given some Christmas leave and we went there as also did my father. The three men went off shooting wild peafowl, which were over-abundant and annoying the villagers by gobbling up their crops. For our Christmas dinner we had roast peacock and it was very tasty.

The Cawnpore Zenana Hospital for women patients only, agreed that I should have my baby there. No males were allowed but Geoffrey was welcomed. He had been in Cawnpore with his parents as a boy at a time when the hospital was plagued by mischievous monkeys. The patients and nurses were being harassed by them and food stolen as the women ate. Geoffrey, then being only a boy, was allowed on the premises and got rid of the monkeys by firing blank cartridges at them and so frightening them away.

Robin was born on the evening of 2 January 1940 and was in a great hurry. The hospital was not expecting me yet and the nurses said I must wait for the lady doctor who was on her rounds. I explained that I could not wait, while the nurses insisted that I must, even trying to hold him back with their hands while we argued. At last Robin and the lady doctor came into my room at the same time! I was glad to see them! She took charge very efficiently and no-one suffered. Geoffrey was able to see his second son before, his leave over, he returned to Purnea where he was now working and my father went with him.

The great Daroga again figured in my life, as my father, whose bearer he was, agreed that he would be the most responsible person to escort little Mike and the *ayah*, Rosalie by train to stay with a married cousin of Geoffrey's. Lois and Gordon were missionaries, living at Dehra Dun, a night's journey from Cawnpore.

They had a son just two weeks older than Mike so it was fun for both boys to have someone to play with.

Three weeks later I too entrained for Dehra with my second baby and enjoyed spending a few days with Lois. After this pleasant visit it was time for me to journey to Purnea - a night and day trip with baby as well as toddler.

It was now February and Geoffrey was ordered by our Maharaja, his employer, to organise a buffalo shoot. The Maharaja of Bikaner was keen to have a go at the wild buffalo in this region. An empty palace, last lent by our Maharaja to the Marquis of Clydesdale and his team when they made their flight over Everest, was put at their disposal. Geoffrey was in charge, accompanying the party, and so had to leave me at home.

It so happened that a pair of leopards had taken to prowling round our bungalow at night, fresh pug marks being found in the mornings. With Geoffrey away and the servants sleeping in their quarters some distance from the bungalow, I felt a little nervous that night, having heard that babies and dogs were relished by leopards.

At bed time I gathered up my two small boys, the cat and the three dogs into my bedroom. I placed Geoffrey's shotgun with both barrels loaded with SG beside my bed and went to sleep. I was woken in the small hours by a growling sound that came from just outside the door to the veranda. I picked up the gun, cocked it and sat there pointing it towards the veranda door for what seemed like hours until the sound stopped. I did not go to sleep again that night.

When the bearer came in with my morning tea I told him I must have guards with guns the next night. He looked at me in amazement. 'Memsahib' he said, 'you had two men sleeping outside your door last night on the Sahib's orders.' I then realised it had been their snores that had kept me awake most of the night. I also realised how stupid I had been. The dogs would never have slept so peacefully if leopards had been just outside the door. On the other hand, the guards were not exactly alert so the gun might have been useful.

The shoot for His Highness of Bikaner went off successfully. Geoffrey was praised and presented with a silver cigarette box ornamented with the Bikaner crest, which he was honoured to receive. If anyone who reads this is utterly appalled at the shooting of peafowl, crocodile and buffalo, please remember how different the world was then, especially in India. Jungle areas were plentiful, wild animals abounded and it was the people who needed help either for themselves, their crops or their livestock. Geoffrey did shoot both leopards because they were killing goats and calves someone's livelihood - having left a jungle habitat on finding easier prey.

15
Geoffrey Joins Up
(to Belgaum, Quetta & Iraq)

March 1940 brought Geoffrey orders to report to Calcutta for duty prior to proceeding to Belgaum, near Poona, the Army Officers' Training School. Because he had served, though only as a trooper, in the Bihar Light Horse Territorials, he was to get a commission. Written orders informed him that 'no wives, children, dogs or other pets' could accompany him. So we packed up again, this time with many doubts about the future and difficult decisions, with Geoffrey off in one direction far to the west of India, while I and the boys went east. The manager of a sugar factory about twenty miles away kindly offered to store our furniture until we should need it again. Again I was bound for Shillong, my father having found accommodation for me as a paying guest in the house of the British Police sergeant. His wife and I got on very well as she had a small girl, happy to have Mike to play with. There I stayed until Geoffrey's training was over and he was posted to the 2nd/7th Gurkha Rifles at Chaman, on the Afghan border near Quetta.

A new kind of life began as I was allowed to go to Quetta and allotted quarters. First, of course, another long journey faced me; Shillong is not far from India's border with Burma, its north-east frontier, while Quetta is in the extreme north-west, about 2,000 miles apart.

Obviously I must cut down on my entourage; first on dogs. Susie had died while we were still in Purnea and someone there had taken over Willie the cat, whose full name was Wallis Warfield Wilberforce Wills, which dated him. I still had Quaker and Toby. My father agreed to keep Quaker but I did take Toby. My *ayah* Rosalie, a woman from Bihar, could not face going so far from home and I acquired Lydia, a Khasi girl, who had never left Shillong before. The women of the Khasi hills are much more independent than their sisters in the plains. A Mongoloid and matriarchal folk - the women owning the property; the inheritance going from youngest daughter to youngest daughter. The girls may have as many lovers as they wish until they marry, after that they must remain faithful to their husbands. Lydia was ready to travel to the other side of India and the boys took to her. I now had Geoffrey's bearer from his bachelor days, who was named Bengali, although he came from Bihar.

This was the longest till now of all my journeys in India and I had two boys, inexperienced servants plus a dog of which I was in charge. It involved two changes of train at Lucknow and Lahore - thankfully these did connect correctly. Somehow we got to Quetta with no disasters and there Geoffrey met me. He had

Michael and Robin (Charles) with bearer Bengali

been given a few days' leave, which we spent in the Chiltan Hotel, before he had to return to the Afghan border at Chaman, via the Khojak Pass.

I moved with the children into a quarter and found we had been given half a house, which consisted of a sitting room, bathroom and two Wana huts. After the terrible Quetta earthquake, which occurred at night causing enormous casualties, the Army did not allow anyone to sleep inside brick houses. As bedrooms we were given these Wana huts which consisted of windowless mud walls, chest high and topped by tent roofs. Dark and cold in the chilly winters. After giving the boys their hot baths before bedtime they had to be swaddled in blankets and taken outdoors to this strange sleeping accommodation. Luckily one can become used to anything and it became quite normal to go to bed via the garden.

This life continued for about two months; Geoffrey getting an odd day off to visit us when he could get transport. I got in one weekend visit to him. A friend, Daphne, was engaged to Edward, a Lieutenant in the 7th Gurkha Rifles and he and Geoffrey were lent the Rest House by the Quetta side of the Pass, so Daphne and I joined them as I was to chaperone Daphne, who would never have been permitted to visit Edward otherwise. A friend took over my children and we had a blissful weekend - I don't think I was a good duenna.

Michael in Gurkha uniform at Quetta, aged 3½

At last, just before Christmas 1940, the battalion was moved from Chaman to Quetta itself. We were given a newly built, anti-earthquake bungalow, not far from the lines, by a road junction called 'Seven Streams'; not as beautiful or romantic a place as it sounds, but a point in Quetta's irrigation system. Little rain falls round there, so to keep the area watered, ditches were laid and water was piped from far away and led to these drains. There was a strict timetable; water being laid on at a certain time for a particular area. A garden would perhaps get two hours water once a week and that garden would be flooded. It was all well-ordered in good Army style. My boys loved it when it was our garden's turn and they could paddle and splash about while the water gushed in. 'Seven Streams' was the principal junction for this water supply.

It was as well for us that we were moved to our new quarter, as it now got very cold and we could have fires in our bedrooms. It was a great life for the children with parties galore and Father Christmas arriving on a camel. I was able to hire a donkey for Mike to ride; Robin, not quite a year old, was too young for this.

It was as social for the adults too, with dancing at the Club to a real band - to me this was a most glamorous sight with British and Indian officers in a gorgeous variety of full dress uniforms; ladies far more elegantly dressed than I was too. It must have looked somewhat like the night before Waterloo. In fact the emotion at the time was rather the same. The 'phoney' war was still on but everyone expected the men to be sent overseas soon. It looked like a choice between the Western Desert and Malaya and must come before long, so all enjoyed themselves while they could. Geoffrey and I were not left together long. He was sent off on a Small Arms course to Saugor in Central India at the beginning of 1941.

Soon after he had left Robin became ill and was kept in hospital. Measles and pneumonia were diagnosed; nurses were scarce so I was given a private room and told to nurse him myself, in quarantine. A letter came from Geoffrey; he'd found friends stationed at Saugor who invited our whole family to come and stay while Geoffrey was there. Sadly I had to refuse as I was nursing Robin. Mike was staying with a friend. The day Robin and I got home Mike was returned to me with the news that he had measles too, so I had him to nurse as well. After that I got measles myself, and really badly, so it was not a cheerful time. It was also bitterly cold.

We had bought a small car, being, I think, its eighteenth owner. This I had to get pushed up onto our narrow veranda each night, after emptying the radiator to stop it freezing and covering it with a rug. It was a really biting cold due to what was known as the Khojak wind, bearing down on us from the icy mountains of Afghanistan.

We were not left for very long together when Geoffrey did return from Saugor. Word came that the Brigade was to stand ready for departure; no idea of where or when, and we were under the strictest of orders not to let anyone know leaving was imminent. Not until they had left could anyone be told. I could then telegraph my father who wired back that he would rent a house for us. This time there was no packing up of furniture as Quetta shopkeepers had an excellent system of hiring furniture. You walked round the storerooms, picked the items you would like, found what it would cost per month, chose something cheaper and so on till you had what you needed. If after a month or so you got tired of something you could change it for something else. That part was easy. I only had to give the traders a date to take it all away.

What was not so easy was getting everything paid, until I could sell the car. As a second lieutenant Geoffrey had no marriage or child allowance - this was not allowed until he was thirty. We were still expected to run a staffed household and pay Mess bills. I also had to pay off the magnificent Pathan bearer, well-used to looking after uniforms, who Geoffrey was expected to have. Also the *ayah*, Lydia, as she had decided to stay with the bearer. I could not blame her; he was tall, handsome with a wonderful moustache, quite different from the small men of the Khasi hills.

Eventually, debts all paid, I entrained to go back across India to Shillong. This journey was not so easy; what had been promised as a rail connection at Lahore failed. No train was due till next day and I had to take us all to a hotel for the night. I had not budgeted for this and was very worried about whether we would have enough money even for food for the rest of the journey. I was more than thankful to know that my father was waiting for us in Shillong. I got there with less than ten rupees in the world, under fifteen shillings in those days (75 pence now) - no money left but no debts either. Before I left Quetta I had been shocked to hear that some officers had left without paying people like the *dhobi*, washerman and such like.

Still not knowing where Geoffrey had gone, I soon learned. The Colonel had promised to send his wife a telegram wishing their daughter a happy birthday if it was the Western Desert; to his son if it was Malaya. When the telegram came it was to his newly born baby, not a year old. News had broken of the Rashid Ali rebellion in Iraq, so we guessed it was probably Basra that was their destination. Basically it was an internal rebellion stirred up by the Germans, with oil as the prize. It was in the Allies' interest to assist the Iraqi Government. Whilst the Brigade fought its way through Iraq and into Iran, the Russians were making their way south in order to reach the oil first.

After the war Geoffrey told me how eventually the two forces met up at Kirkuk and the Russians organised a party. Two British officers from every unit were invited. This meant the Colonel, with lots being drawn for the other and Geoffrey was the lucky one. The British were given a warm welcome by their Russian hosts but they could speak no Russian and very few Russians spoke English. At dinner the British and Russians were seated alternately; it was very quiet at first but as the drink, principally vodka, flowed it was amazing how everyone began to chat cheerfully to their neighbours. The Russians were well organised for when any officer collapsed at the table a stretcher party of women soldiers immediately removed either guest or host for attention.

As the Brigade had progressed northwards through Iraq I was surprised to find how religious Geoffrey's letters to me had become. He urged me to read certain passages from the Old Testament. I realised, quite quickly, that if I did I could plot his way through places like Ur of Chaldees and other biblical towns, and find out whereabouts he had been.

Robin at Shillong, aged 2

16
To Shillong
1941-1942

Arriving again in Shillong I found that my father had been able to rent a bungalow on the side of a hill with quite a steep drive up to it. He had chosen very cleverly as there were two wings with a small study, his bedroom and bathroom on the side. A dining and sitting room connected them to my wing with a small sitting room for me and three bedrooms. This gave him privacy and I had a bedroom for myself, another for the boys and a playroom for them. It was sparsely furnished but my father had solved that problem. He sent that stalwart of a bearer, Daroga, off to where we had been prior to Geoffrey's call up to collect all our furniture from where it was stored.

It was a pleasant surprise to see our household belongings again and know they were safe. Certain items were missing; none of our brass oil lamps had come. When I asked about them Daroga explained that since Shillong had electricity the oil lamps were not needed. This was true, but a few years later we did need them and were never able to find such beautiful brass ones again. I also noticed that a round chased brass table top had not been brought either, nor some brass ash trays. Obviously Daroga did not like brass; he must have had to polish a lot over his years of service, but he had done an excellent job collecting our possessions and getting them packed up and transported by lorry, train and ferry and then another long drive to reach Shillong safely. I could not complain, especially when I realised that Daroga had first come to work as a young boy to help my mother with her cultivation of silkworms and the spinning of silk, before I was born. He had received no formal education but had progressed to being the head of my father's household and continued with him on his retirement. He had become well-travelled, having done train journeys all over India.

My father told me how, when he was engaging a cook and other servants for this rented bungalow, when each applicant produced his reference or chitties, Daroga would hand them on to my father. As he did so, Daroga would say scornfully, 'I have no chitties and will never have a chitty.' Having worked for my father all his life this was so and he was proud of it. He died some years later, still in my father's service.

Now I had to engage an *ayah*. Through a lady with whom I had lodged when in Shillong earlier, I was lucky enough to meet Ka (Mrs) Nadybon Kharkongar, who agreed to come and look after my children. Nadybon had three grown up daughters, Rellis, Tellis and Robbis, and a younger son, Redily. Khasis like giving their families rhyming names. Later I was to know of two notorious sisters, Million and Billion. This was around 1941 and Nadybon stayed with me until 1956. I was even able to keep in touch with her until her death.

The war had not yet impinged greatly on Shillong society, tucked away, as we were, in the furthest corner of north-east India. Only those with husbands fighting really knew there was a war on. It stayed like that until Singapore was taken by the Japanese. The Allied troops were forced to retreat all the way through Burma and into India.

Early in 1942 these poor men made their weary way into safety, most in a terrible condition suffering from malnutrition, malaria, dysentery and jungle sores as well as wounds. They had been strafed all the time by Japanese planes and there were no Allied aircraft to combat this. Many of them were sent to Shillong, only a small hill station, which was totally unprepared for the influx. There were insufficient hospitals, but senior officers gave up their big bungalows for this use. Ladies like myself, who had done any kind of nursing, were co-opted. We were told to get white dresses made and white muslin squares to wear on our heads, as nurses did in those days. It was not difficult to get these uniforms made, with plenty of white cotton material, no coupons needed and numerous tailors, or *darzies*.

In order to maintain order among men who were somewhat undisciplined after what they had gone through, we were called 'sisters' and had to behave as such. The men that I was helping to look after were mainly suffering from jungle sores, malaria and dysentery. I was used to coping with the latter two but did find the former really unpleasant.

I, and others like me, were working in one of the converted bungalows; really serious cases went to what hospitals there were. A doctor made his rounds daily but otherwise we had to manage on our own. There were men from two particular regiments in my care, one from northern England and the other Scottish. No names of these regiments, which I could give, so no pack drill as they say. Sadly the English patients were not pleasing to nurse. I knew they had had a terrible time and was ready to help them but their attitude to me meant I had to screw up all my courage to enter their rooms. Changing their dressings was an ordeal because of the way they treated us, obviously resenting anyone in authority.

On the other hand the Scots, who had suffered just as badly, were a pleasure to help; such appreciative patients, always offering to help us.

"Can I no' carry that tray for you, Sister." "Let me help with ma bed, Sister."

Such a contrast, leaving me with such a lasting and happy memory of them, whilst I prefer to forget the others. As soon as possible, the real Queen Alexandra Nurses arrived and took over from us. I was sorry as I had felt I had been doing something worthwhile, even if not always enjoyable.

I began to be bombarded with letters from Geoffrey and from his parents in England, urging me to take the two boys away from what was thought to be a danger zone with the enemy advancing steadily to India. Geoffrey was by now in the Western Desert, the Iraqi campaign being over and he had become worried about our safety. The Japs were by then only about fifty miles away by air, though a lot further by road through difficult mountain terrain.

I did have somewhere to which I could retreat as his parents owned an empty bungalow in the Kumaon Hills near Naini Tal, a centrally located part of northern India. It was a fruit orchard and a fine place for children. Against my own wishes and better judgement I gave in, just in case I was endangering my children unnecessarily.

My father stayed put, especially since he had set up an amenities store for the Indian soldiers in Shillong. Shillong did already have an Indian Military Hospital as some Indian troops, mainly Gurkhas, had been stationed there always. That hospital was kept for them.

17
War Work in Shillong
(Geoffrey taken prisoner at Tobruk)

Many of the British ladies, especially those with small children, had decided it was wise to leave. Military families were given railway warrants - a great help. Off I set again, an experienced train traveller by now, but it was not a comfortable journey as it was May and the temperature was 120°F. With war on India's Eastern front there were massive troop movements, luckily going the opposite way to us. Also the Indian Congress was causing uprisings against Government. It was not an easy journey and I had to make a night stop in a hotel in Lucknow; this time I was prepared so it was a pleasant break and we were able to have baths!

Nadybon was a stalwart soul and agreed to come with me as long as her daughter, Tellis, could come too, neither having left Shillong before. Daroga's son, Jibach, had become my bearer as Daroga himself would no longer leave my father.

I have a vague memory of taking the boys then aged four and two to Lucknow Zoo to give them an outing before another train journey in the evening. Then it was on again for the railhead for the Kumaon Hills. A hired car took us to the point beyond which it was not motorable, from there only a track existed leading to the bungalow, perched on a hillside looking onto the lower slopes of the Himalayas.

Carrying-chairs, called *dandies*, were provided for Nadybon and Tellis and another was shared by the boys. Jibach and I rode and all our baggage was carried by porters. My dog Toby ran alongside, delighted to be free again. We made quite a cavalcade going on our way through the hills, the path rising all the way to a completely unknown destination. It took nearly two hours to get to it but it was a beautiful spot; a small bungalow on a spur below the Himalayas and around it apple orchards. It was lovely but I found it very lonely. The British manager of the orchards lived nearer to where we had left the main road and only visited occasionally. He would send on my mail and papers by anyone going that way, also stores when we needed them. We could get basics like rice, flour, sugar and ghee from a shop in a village on a lower slope. There was an elderly British couple living on their own orchard, but about an hour's walk in another direction, so I only visited them once, as it was hard for Mike and Robin needing carrying.

My only other visitor was a British Forest officer who called in whenever he was on tour anywhere nearby and he took us on picnics down to the river far below us. These were great occasions.

To make matters worse for me, when I had not been there very long I got the dreaded telegram saying that Geoffrey was 'missing, believed a Prisoner of

War'. There was no-one to whom I could talk, no way of getting up-to-date information and it was only when the delayed newspapers arrived telling of the fall of Tobruk and of the magnificent fight put up by a Gurkha battalion that I could even guess at what might have happened. It was not easy to try and be cheerful for the sake of my two little boys but it was they that kept me going. For them it was a wonderful place - trees to climb and picnics down the hillside. It was beautiful too; there was a spectacular view down into the valley and across more hills and away to the snowy peaks of mountains in the background - the great range of the Himalayas with Nanda Devi recognisable. All this beauty was lost on me in my misery.

My troubles got worse, not only could I get no news at all about Geoffrey but my dog Toby swallowed the one and only chicken bone of his life; something I had always been careful our dogs should never eat; he soon showed he was in pain. I too was in pain with acute sinus trouble. I sent word to the orchard manager and a posse of *dandies* and ponies arrived to take us all down to his bungalow. He and his wife took us in. Toby was taken to a vet, where he died from a pierced intestine. I was sent to a military hospital in the plains. The world looked bleak.

On my return from hospital I knew I could not stand the loneliness of that hillside bungalow. I contacted old friends from my Bihar days, still working there, who were pleased to join me for a holiday away from the heat and dust of the plains. That made life more bearable but I still could get no word about Geoffrey. When the time came for my friends, the Hickeys, to leave I felt I must go with them back to Bihar, where other friends were happy for me and my boys to stay with them.

There was still no news of Geoffrey but events on the Assam front were static; the Japs making no further advances. My father wrote suggesting I should return to Shillong, especially as the Regimental base was there, giving a chance of getting news more quickly. I am sure it was coincidence but I was hardly back when I heard that Geoffrey was indeed a prisoner of war. I was given an address in Italy to which I could write. Also I received a letter from the Vatican telling me that their representative had visited the POW camp at Chieti and had seen Geoffrey who was well and unhurt. All wonderful news but I had had to wait from June to September and I have never known such long months. All of us were happy; my father was glad to have us there with him; the boys pleased and Nadybon and Tellis were home again. Only one person was sad, poor Daroga whose son had started work as my bearer but had been caught stealing money when I was staying with my Bihar friends. His home town was nearby and I sent him back there. I felt so sorry for Daroga.

At last, completing my happiness, came letters from Geoffrey himself. He kept asking after our dog Toby and I could not bring myself to let him know Toby was dead, he had been so fond of him; and so the questions continued, unanswered. We now had no pets at all, until I was asked to look after Roger, a spaniel whose master was off into the fighting in Burma. I was told by his master before he left that Roger had been given an anti-rabies vaccination, valid for the next six months.

The six months can hardly have passed before I found Roger foaming at the mouth, a sign of rabies. Carefully putting on gloves I took Roger to the vet. In order to be certain it was rabies, he was put in a cage, because a rabid dog does not live for more than a few days. Sadly Roger was dead a day later, a case of dumb rabies. Shillong had one of the few Pasteur Institutes and the dog's brain was examined there and rabies confirmed. As a result, all of the household who had handled Roger in the past few days had to have the full treatment of fourteen injections into our stomachs, including poor little Robin only just three years old. It was then I was told by the doctor at the Pasteur Institute that Geoffrey should never keep a dog after his experience when he had to have this treatment, as he could be allergic. Luckily the rest of us had no problems bar our sore tummies.

Much had changed in Shillong in my absence; soldiers of many kinds were stationed there: British, Indian, American and even Nigerians. Some American mounted troops had a camp not far from Shillong itself. My sons, now middle-aged men, still remember them because they put on rodeo shows. They had seen such things on films but to see the real thing was something they have not forgotten. It was something many of us enjoyed.

There were now convalescent camps and rest camps for the men fighting in the Burma campaign, giving them much needed breaks. This led to many canteens and I was asked to help with an RAF depot canteen, which I did for some months.

I had considered joining the Women's Auxiliary Corps (India) and going into uniform, but with small children I did not want to be tied to a job when they needed me, or be liable to be sent elsewhere. Then a WAC(I) friend came to me for help. She needed an operation and her Commandant said she must take leave for this. Pat wanted to save her leave till her husband, overseas like mine, could get back and they could both be free. Then her Commandant said that if she could find someone to take her place she could go and have her operation. India is a great country for the 'badli', the replacer; I am not sure if this could have been done elsewhere. When Pat asked if I would be her 'badli' I was glad to do it. When I reported for duty I was not sent to where she had been working. Instead I went to work at the Station Staff Office in company with some Indian civilian clerks. At last my typing ability was of real use and I preferred this to my canteen duties. When Pat recovered and was back at work it did not seem to make any difference to what I had been doing.

On asking the Station Staff Officer if he would like me to carry on he said he would ask Area Headquarters if I could be put on his staff officially. This would mean I could be paid which would be a great help. Unfortunately HQ refused. They wrote that unless I became a WAC(I) I could not be employed; no civilian ladies were permitted and my 'services were to be dispensed with forthwith'.

This seemed absurd! If Indian civilian clerks could be employed, why not British civilian ladies? But rules were rules and the young British officer who was SSO had to obey, but only up to a point. I had felt disappointed having enjoyed doing a proper job, so I asked if he would like me to continue unofficially. He accepted my offer gladly and took a delight in personally typing out a letter saying that my services had been dispensed with as ordered, even typing in my initials as typist.

Every morning the 15cwt Army truck collected me with the WAC(I) girls and left me at my office, where I continued to work contentedly with my clerical friends under the command of the SSO.

After a few weeks, the entire office personnel, myself with them, were moved into part of the Sub-Area HQ's office, under the command of a Brigadier. He was a darling and used to pop his head into my office every day with a cheery 'Good morning', and yet I was never there officially.

I was given files with big red crosses on the cover, marked 'Most Secret', which I treated with extra care. One of these showed the site of every unit in the area. I returned this as soon as possible while a Colonel left it on his desk during lunch and it disappeared. I panicked, wondering if they would blame me and I would be shot as a spy, but all was well; it had fallen into a waste paper basket.

Most of the work was done directly with the most efficient Warrant Officer, who turned out later to be a real friend in need. The only times I was ever present officially was as typist for a couple of Courts-Martial. One was a very ordinary case about what a drunken British other rank had said to a senior officer. Although the words used should be unprintable, they had to be written down. They were new to me, I had led a sheltered life, so I asked my father how to spell them. He was most upset that his innocent daughter should be hearing such language!

The other case was more amusing; a British soldier had been caught 'Out of Bounds' by the Military Police in the home of a notorious Khasi girl. He was imprisoned in a corrugated iron roofed cell. Million, the lady in question, was allowed to visit him and passed him a tin opener with which he cut his way out through the roof, absconding with Million into the Khasi hills. Foolishly, while he was there he met Million's sister, Billion, and turned his attentions to her, whereupon Million, a woman scorned, informed the Military Police of his whereabouts and he was back in jail.

He told me that he did not really mind if he spent the rest of the war in the 'Glasshouse'. He was safe there and would sit out the war until he could cash in some jewellery he had pinched on his way out of Burma and had stashed away.

18
Geoffrey's Escape

At last a happier day dawned for me - in December 1943 I had a telegram to say that Geoffrey had escaped and reached the Allied lines in Italy. The most wonderful news! Next came a telegram from Geoffrey himself to say he was in Cairo but being sent back to India. This was followed by another from Delhi telling me to expect him any moment. I abandoned my work, with the Brigadier's blessing; not that he could object since I had never been there officially.

Haunting the Transit Depot, scanning every vehicle that arrived there, I still managed to miss the moment he did turn up. A friend, learning who he was, brought him straight home to me. He arrived on December 23, so you can imagine what a wonderful Christmas that was. I was in such a flutter I put the small silver trinkets for the Christmas pudding into the Christmas cake which made it dangerous eating! Nobody cared.

Geoffrey was given three months' leave. It was a marvellous time for us all and he was there for Michael's sixth birthday and Robin's fourth; both in January, and was their best birthday present.

Although thin, Geoffrey was in a reasonable state of health after fifteen months as a POW and nearly three months working his way through Italy. He vowed he would never fuss over his food again! When walking to the bazaar, the odd chicken would cross in front of us and Geoffrey said it was quite difficult for him to restrain himself from catching it! They were food. I think this feeling never quite left him; he was never greedy, nor did he overeat, but he was always keen to shoot, fish and collect whatever food was available, such as mushrooms, nuts and berries, shrimps, prawns, crabs or other edibles.

Geoffrey's adventures should have had a book to themselves but he was not a man to sit still long enough to write his story. Neither did he ever want to talk much about it; what I learned was mainly in bits and pieces on different occasions, which I have managed to collate.

Geoffrey was taken prisoner when Tobruk fell to the Germans in 1942. It became public knowledge that the 2/7th Gurkha Rifles, with whom he was serving, fought on for twenty-four hours after the rest of Tobruk surrendered, until they had no ammunition left. The Germans treated them with the respect they deserved and apologised for having to hand them over to the Italians, as they, the Germans, must get on with the war.

The Italians did not behave so well, as they stripped their prisoners of any valuables. Geoffrey thus lost his gold signet ring and his watch. He lost something else - his shot gun - because the Colonel, keen to shoot any game going, told Geoffrey to bring his shot gun when they left India. While in Iraq and Iran this had been useful as they shot sand grouse among other game, making their rations tastier. Not knowing what to do with his gun he buried it in a slit trench in Tobruk as he did not want the enemy to have it. It may still be lying there in the sand with, possibly, a tourist hotel built above it.

After being shipped across to Italy they arrived at a prisoner of war camp at Chieti. There Geoffrey spent much of his time tunnelling. The Italians actually gave their prisoners permission to start a vegetable garden to augment their rations. This was most useful for disposing of the soil from the tunnels, carried out in their trouser legs and scattered as they walked up and down their plot. When the height of the earth grew too much the Italians did get suspicious and began stringent searching. One tunnel did get used but Geoffrey did not draw one of the lucky straws. Another tunnel, which was under the stove in Geoffrey's own quarters, was never discovered.

Tunnelling became more dangerous and difficult and his friends tried to persuade Geoffrey to learn to play bridge to pass the time. He preferred tunnelling and map-making.

Eventually the Italians surrendered to the Allies in the autumn of 1943 and Chieti camp was abandoned by them, leaving everything behind. Most of the Allied officers then wanted to make their own way out to freedom. Unfortunately the senior British officer ordered no-one to leave the camp and even posted his own officers with Italian weapons to mount guard and prevent anyone leaving. He had the mistaken belief that the Allies would soon be there and he could hand over an orderly camp.

Very soon the Germans had surrounded the camp and decided to move the prisoners to Germany. First they were taken to an old and dilapidated transit camp at Sulmona, the buildings of which were in such a tumble-down state that a few of the doors had been bricked up. Geoffrey and three others saw possibilities there and discovered an old and apparently unused latrine. Collecting up what food and water they could, they bricked themselves up into this rather unsavoury shelter.

Others had also tried to hide and the Germans, finding themselves short of several prisoners, began to blow up some of the buildings, calling out warnings before they did so. When it came to the building next to theirs and warnings were called out of more bombing to come, Geoffrey and his pals gave up; it was silly to get blown up. They had spent three days in that smelly dump to no purpose except that they found themselves even more closely guarded as known escapers.

When put on a train next day, probably bound for Colditz, they found armed guards sitting, guns ready, in the doorways at each end of the long carriage. But Geoffrey was not one to give up hope. At a railway station he managed to attract the attention of the very brave Italian Station Master, who succeeded in passing in a key to their compartment door. Geoffrey and his friend, Frank Stone, twisted the light bulbs to break the connection, then at a suitable moment as darkness fell the train began to slow down on the incline of an embankment of a bridge. They seized their chance, opened the door and jumped. Rolling down the bank, shots going over their heads and expecting the train to stop; somehow they reached cover and tore away into comparative safety. Possibly the train did not stop because it was already partly on the bridge or perhaps the driver wanted to get home, anyhow they were lucky as there was no-one chasing them.

From the attitude of the Station Master they felt the Germans were not popular and Italian villagers might give them some help. They made their way cautiously; dusk had fallen and lights appeared not too far away, indicating a village of some kind. Making their way silently they hid in thick bushes where they spent the night. As soon as it was light they watched for movements. No German troops could they see but noticed a priest emerging from his home. He seemed the most likely source of help, but they stayed in hiding until it was dark again and then crept up to his house. He fed them and hid them long enough for them to make maps of that area, moving on as they did not want to endanger him any longer.

Later on they came across charcoal burners in some woodland who helped them on their way, giving them a little food to take with them. But for the food from them and the priest they only had raw vegetables dug from fields at night. No cooking was possible as they feared a fire would give them away. In a forest further south they met up with a group of escaped Gurkha soldiers from their own regiment, the 2/7th Gurkha Rifles. When they had all been taken prisoner at Tobruk the officers had been taken off separately and had been kept under strict guard. The men had been allowed to work in the fields and had got friendly with villagers. Now free from German supervision they were living in these woods, very well-organised under their Subedar Major, a senior Viceroy's-commissioned officer, and still helping and being helped by local Italians. Geoffrey and Frank were pressed by the Subedar Major to remain with them, sure as they were that the Allied forces would reach them soon; but they decided to continue south.

After much hardship they reached the mountains overlooking Cassino, with its magnificent monastery, the battle for which was in progress. Another British officer and a Gurkha soldier had joined Frank and Geoffrey; life was hard for them all. They remained in the mountains although it was now November and very cold, because there were German troops ahead between them and the Allies.

They fed themselves on cattle and sheep that had been killed by shellfire. After dark they would collect the meat. Geoffrey was nearly caught on one of these expeditions. He was coming down a narrow hill track carrying the meat in a battered tin bowl, a tattered civilian overcoat over his shoulders hiding his uniform, when he came face to face with a German patrol. Stepping to the edge of the path he bowed his head politely and wished them good day in Italian. They hesitated, gave a grunt and continued on their way; the heavy rain and awful conditions together with Geoffrey's scruffy appearance, shaggy hair and tangled beard obviously saved him. Probably the Germans wanted to get to their billets, hot food and a warm fire and decided action was pointless. Another day the four of them were surprised by a single German soldier testing telephone lines. Overcoming him, they removed his boots, braces, belt and ammunition but not his gun. Leaving him they told him where he could find his clothes and ammunition further ahead. They did not take his gun away as they realised he would have to report his loss, instead they hoped he would keep quiet so as not to look foolish. In any case if they had been caught and found to be armed they were liable to be shot outright.

So far they had been lucky; life was hard but they were still free, until the day when a full patrol came on them suddenly. They had an arrangement whereby each would run in a different direction and put this into practice, scattering to the four points of the compass. The plan was then to return at night to the spot where they had been and to give a special whistle. Geoffrey did this for the next two nights but no-one answered his call. He found a German blood-stained field dressing so knew someone had been hit. It was hopeless to go on waiting but as bad to have to carry on alone.

It was now December and snow was falling. Life in the mountains felt colder and colder and he was becoming more and more hungry. Below him he could see a German camp and beyond that he knew must be the Allied lines. He decided he could stand this no longer and plunged down the slope at nightfall. Snow fell heavily as he trudged on, passing German dugouts, hearing their voices but not stopping until he was well clear of them, then he hid.

It was almost dawn when he saw soldiers in a uniform he could not recognise and remained hidden until an Italian woman came past. Whispering in Italian he asked her what troops they were. 'Americans' she replied. Geoffrey had been taken prisoner soon after the Americans entered the war and so far had not seen their uniforms. On hearing this he ran to a building he had seen not far off. He found the moment of entering the most frightening of all; it was an American Officers' Mess and every man there levelled a handgun at him as he stood in the doorway. Hands above his head he yelled that he was British. After that he could not have been treated with more kindness - almost too kind - stuffing him with food until he was violently sick. A fine American overcoat was given to him, which he kept for many years.

He learned from these Americans that he had walked right through a German minefield and past an American outpost. The occupants of the latter were given a rocket for not spotting him. Soon he was sent on to the British, who had a camp at Bari all prepared to welcome hundreds of escaped prisoners of war and he was the only man to go there. He was overwhelmed with attentions of every kind: bathed, showered, re-clothed and fed with more sense than the Americans, in their kindness, had shown a half-starved man. From there he was flown to the British Headquarters in Cairo, since he had valuable information. He had taken note of all the German gun emplacements which he was able to see as he hid in the mountains overlooking Cassino. Now pinpointed they could be targeted and I am sure this information helped the Allies to win the battle for Cassino.

Geoffrey was awarded a well-deserved Military Cross. Strangely he never received any Citation; during his life he never mentioned this and I never thought about it. After his death in 1988 my two sons asked about this but I knew nothing. Both having Ministry of Defence connections they made enquiries but never learned anything. Was this because the Medal was awarded for actions in secrecy in enemy territory? After the war was over Geoffrey heard that the other three who had been with him had all been captured by the Germans. The Gurkha had been shot and killed and the other two taken prisoner, but Frank had escaped again and this time he had made it and was back home in Ireland. Before Geoffrey was able to meet him again he heard Frank had died.

19
Geoffrey at Imphal
1944

My voluntary work at Sub-Area Headquarters now paid off handsomely as the Warrant Officer, for whom I had been working directly, gave my husband and me considerable help. When the Ministry of Defence tried to make claims on Geoffrey he was able to file even bigger claims against them. He knew every paragraph in King's Regulations and exactly for which entitlements Geoffrey could claim. There was of course the watch and ring the Italians had taken, lost uniform and so on. When the Paymaster's Office claimed for overpaid back pay in 1942 it was pointed out that it was now time-barred!

Geoffrey was helped to fill in all the numerous forms correctly for every possible allowance and compensation permissible. Warrant Officers are experts when it comes to forms. One thing for which Geoffrey could not claim was the shot gun lying buried in Tobruk.

As he had escaped from the Germans, Geoffrey could not be sent to that theatre of war, where other battalions of his Regiment were fighting. When his three months' leave was over at the end of March 1944, Geoffrey was posted to Imphal, on the Indian border with Burma, now in the front line of the war with Japan, as a major with the Assam Rifles.

Before the war these were units in Assam, half-soldiers and half-policemen, whose duty it was to protect India's borders with Tibet and Burma and keep the peace in its tribal areas. The Assam Rifles were composed mainly of Gurkhas, not all born in Nepal, many from Darjeeling and the sons of Gurkha soldiers born in India. They were stationed at various outlying posts on India's boundaries. It was to one of these Geoffrey was now posted.

They were under the command of the Commissioner of Police of Assam Province, who was stationed in Shillong. He was also a golf playing friend of my father and having met Geoffrey and heard his record, Lou Hutchins put in for him to be sent to the 5th Battalion, Assam Rifles, Imphal.

At that time I was pleased as he was not going to be so far away. The Commissioner was driving there himself on a tour of inspection and offered to take Geoffrey with him. Once again he was to have a Commanding Officer keen on shooting, who sent word that Geoffrey should bring a shot gun; the snipe shooting around Imphal was very good.

On their way to Imphal they stopped the night at Kohima, another Assam Rifles outpost. There they learned that the Japs had made big advances and were closing around Imphal, which was likely to be besieged. My father had given

Geoffrey his shot gun to take with him and, not wanting to lose another gun in another siege, he left the gun with the officers in Kohima. Leaving for Imphal in the morning, Geoffrey and the Commissioner got there safely but the latter decided to leave for Shillong immediately. Just as well, as it was not long before the Japs had completely surrounded Imphal.

Once again Geoffrey was under siege; for me this seemed much worse. I did not learn about Tobruk until it was over but I learned all about this, feeling I preferred Geoffrey as a German prisoner of war to a Japanese one, specially hearing that they did not actually take prisoners when fighting.

Geoffrey found this was a very different affair and a more silent one. Not the same violent and noisy attacks with tanks and bombardments, instead it was more like a cat watching a mousehole; they were completely surrounded. At night they would see the glimmer of fires all round and know every move was watched. Frequently a sentry would get nervous and fire at a shadow, whereupon every sentry all round the perimeter would start firing and a fierce fusillade would follow. Probably there was nothing there, but there might have been.

Imphal withstood the siege but it was a nasty time. I dreaded that, having got away from the Germans, he would fall to the Japs. Quite how bad that would have been I could not have imagined at that time. Since then I have visited the real Bridge on the River Kwai, seen the vast cemetery filled with such young men and seen the pictures in the local museum. Thankfully Imphal was too tough and the Japanese turned their attention to the less impregnable Kohima and did manage to overrun it.

The Battle of the Tennis Court, once part of the District Commissioner's garden, has become a part of military history. The tennis court itself is part of a War Graves Cemetery with a memorial to the many who died defending Kohima. A very minor casualty in the fighting was the shot gun; this one never had a burial, neither had Geoffrey needed it to shoot snipe, he was far too busy with heavier artillery and a different target.

At last the enemy was retreating. British and Indian troops had come to Kohima's aid. Lines of communication had opened up and I was able to get news of Geoffrey. He had been sent to reinforce the Assam Rifles battalion in Kohima, which had suffered much. From there he was able to make occasional short trips to Shillong, cadging lifts in military vehicles passing through.

At long last I got permission to pay a weekend visit, going by train from our nearest railhead at Gauhati to Dimapur and then a long drive to Kohima. My return was by the same route, but when I got to Dimapur to catch the evening train it had been cancelled. The station master was kind enough to lend me his office table to sleep on. It was not quite long enough but greatly preferable to the dirty concrete floor.

I spent more time travelling than in Kohima but still felt it had been worthwhile. I also saw the immediate effects of war at first hand; the once densely-wooded hills around Kohima were now a few scattered trees standing like skeletons over singed undergrowth; shattered buildings being hastily patched up; even a Jap skull half hidden under fallen debris.

Among the repaired buildings was the Assam Rifles Officers' Mess, where I was put up. It had been mended by stretching lengths of coarse hessian between bamboo poles and painting the material with liquid cement. This hardened and made an excellent wall.

Both Imphal and Kohima were in the territory of the Nagas, although under the jurisdiction of the Governor of Assam. These people were head hunters; a Naga boy was not considered to be a man until he had taken a head. Because the women and children were more closely-guarded and kept nearer their homes, their heads were considered better prizes as, being more difficult to get, they gave their taker more kudos. The British government had been trying to stamp out this vicious way of life. Now they relaxed, having no objection to Japanese heads being taken, and the Nagas were rewarded for these.

The District Commissioner Mr Pawsey, in whose garden was sited the famous tennis court and to whom the heads were taken, decreed that a pair of ears, rather than a complete head, was enough evidence.

The Nagas gave the Allies great help in the war against the Japanese, slipping silently through their familiar jungles and taking the enemy by surprise. When Geoffrey was ordered to take a patrol of Assam Riflemen into Burma he took Nagas as guides.

The Americans had set up, or rather dropped, listening posts in North Burma; the operators and their equipment having been parachuted in. It was to these posts Geoffrey and his men had to visit, all on foot through difficult jungle terrain.

I knew little about this or its true purpose as it was a secret mission. Beyond telling me it had been an interesting trip, Geoffrey would say no more. Later, when presumably he could have gone into detail, we had both forgotten all about it - too busy leading normal, happy lives.

20
Canteen Lady, Shillong
1944-1945

While Geoffrey was occupied as I have described, I was doing what I could to help the war effort. A Garrison Theatre was nearing completion; until now the only cinema was the small, pre-war place in the town, quite unable to cope with the crowd of servicemen wanting entertainment. The new building was badly needed as there was little recreation for men while recuperating from wounds or disease, or having a much-deserved break from the stress of jungle warfare.

Included was an area for a canteen and I was appointed to organise this and I wanted it to be different. No 'chai' - the tea, sugar and milk were to be served separately, unlike elsewhere. A cup of tea, to which my customers could help themselves to their taste of sugar and/or milk could be had from our counter. Our pots of tea, served with milk jugs and sugar bowls could be served at tables. I did not rely on voluntary help; it was too unreliable for the best of reasons, such as a sick child. I engaged a cook, two bearers who served the tables and a small boy. It was his job to produce toast, which he did crouched at the cook's foot in front of the glowing bars of the iron range. Hot buttered toast became very popular and not to be had elsewhere.

As this canteen was part of the Garrison Theatre it was open to all ranks and their civilian friends. Thus both officers and other ranks could use the canteen and offer their friends a 'cuppa'. This was something I felt made a pleasant atmosphere and it seemed to work smoothly.

We were only open in the mornings, closing during the matinée and opening again between that and the evening performance. This meant a supper was available before the last show and I would always have a hot dish ready. A favourite item was roast pork and much disappointment was caused when it had to come off the menu. Officialdom disapproved of it as unhealthy. Evidently they just looked at the pigs running about in the bazaar eating scraps. My pigs came from a well-run farm from which I had got pork for a long time.

Once a month the Brigadier, for whom I had worked earlier and who had appointed me, held a meeting of Canteen Managers, such as the lady who ran the Dew Drop Inn canteen. I was not liked by them; they criticised my tea arrangements and hot toast as being wasteful but, while I made no profits for charity, I made no losses and carried on.

Two sergeants were in charge of the Garrison Theatre itself and the running of the films. Really nice men who encouraged me to bring my small sons with me and kept an eye on them when I was extra busy. Once they took them off in the 15cwt when collecting supplies, to have a ride, leaving a frantic mama hunting for her children. After that time they did always tell me first.

Stars to entertain the troops paid short visits and I had to provide their snacks in the intervals. Only one left a lasting impression - Margaret Lockwood, who was so beautiful.

The canteen service at the Garrison Theatre, Shillong
(Felicity, née Anderson, serving)

There was one special occasion when General (later Viscount) Slim wanted the European civilians of Shillong to become more conscious that 'Careless talk costs lives'. The film 'In Which We Serve' was then on view at the Garrison Theatre and the General decided they should all see this and be addressed by him, with a tea provided afterwards. This affected both the sergeants and me as everything needed to be tuned exactly for smooth efficiency.

We ran through the time the film took, how long Bill Slim took over his address and he was good enough to rehearse this for us to time it until we had it all exactly right. This was most necessary for me; I needed to know just when to pour the boiling water on to the tea leaves and serve the large crowd who had come, both to meet the General and see the show. Complimenting me at the end and being an ex-7th Gurkha officer, he asked where Geoffrey was. Having heard his address and seen the film so many times I had become so imbued with security that, without thinking, I said 'I can't tell you that'. Then I realised to whom I was speaking and began an embarrassed apology. The General cut me short, 'It's I who should apologise. I should not have asked you that, but I hope all's well with him.' I was able to say that, as far as I knew, it was.

Everything went on without bother and with satisfied customers, but Authority thought more was needed. Another building was being erected next door. It was to be a Soldiers' Club, with facilities we could not provide, and to be run by TocH and open every day. When completed, our little effort was moved into the new building but it never seemed the same again. I admit prejudice but there was no longer the mixture of all ranks and their civilian friends which I had encouraged.

It just so happened that volunteers were wanted for a new canteen to be opened in Kohima. I volunteered at once, knowing my sons would be safe with their Grandfather and Nadybon, the *ayah*. I was accepted and sent to a Forces medical officer to have all my jabs and joined the queue of men waiting. I noticed some odd looks but thought nothing of it. My turn came and I had the necessary inoculations; I also discovered I had been in the 'FFI' parade. 'FFI' meant 'Free from Infection' and I leave you to guess just what infection the Medical Officer was looking for. Very embarrassing when I realised. On top of that I never got to Kohima as I had hoped, because the Area Commander discovered I had a husband there. No wives were to be allowed - this gave me to wonder what other duties were expected. I had handed over charge to the TocH representative but carried on helping. Luckily he and I got on well but I was no longer really needed; I would never have volunteered for Kohima otherwise.

Eventually the theatre of war moved eastwards as the enemy were driven back out of Burma, then Malaya; the Indian frontier was no longer threatened.

The Assam Rifles did not move out of Assam, and Kohima now could have numbers cut down, so Geoffrey was loaned to the Political Service. He became an Assistant Political Officer in Sadiya, a histrict headquarters on the banks of the Brahmaputra River, where it pours out from the mountains of Tibet. It was a very interesting assignment as Geoffrey now dealt with tribal people, the Abors and the Mishmis who lived among the hills up to the border. It also meant he would now have a bungalow and I, and the children, could and did join him.

21

To Sadiya, North-East Frontier
(Geoffrey in the Political Service)

On his arrival in Sadiya, Geoffrey was to report to the Political Officer at his bungalow. He found his new boss, 'Johnnie' (G.E.D. Walker), laid up with a badly cut foot. He also met the other Assistant Political Officer, Peter, who was visiting and learned that he was in charge of the more distant Abor territory, while Geoffrey was to remain in Sadiya with the Mishmi area to look after. He also learned how Johnnie had come to cut his foot. When Peter came with his reports he had brought some Abors with him. They were great dancers and in showing Johnnie a particular dance requiring much twirling of *daos* (knives which all tribal people carried), Peter had joined in. Not as proficient as the Abors, his *dao* had slipped from his hand and gone spinning across the room. Johnnie had put out his foot in an effort to stop it slashing into his radiogram, his most precious possession. The *dao* sliced into his foot instead and he nearly lost his toes. *Daos* are kept very sharp.

At that time there was an American unit in Sadiya who ran a generator and allowed the Political Officers to have a little electricity in their bungalows. Johnnie reserved most of his for his radiogram, with one light as well. He was at least able to listen to music while his foot healed. When I got there we did without radio and music, preferring extra lights in our small bungalow close to the banks of the Brahmaputra river.

Peter managed the Abor tribes in the hills to the north-west while Geoffrey had the Mishmi to look after in the eastern hills and also the plains area round the headquarters at Sadiya. Johnnie was in overall charge of the whole district.

Assamese was the official language, so Geoffrey learned that in addition to the Hindi and Gurkhali, and some Italian, that he already spoke. There was even a battalion of the Assam Rifles stationed on border security. A new Colonel from a Gurkha battalion had recently been posted there and had brought his old Gurkha orderly with him; they had both been serving in Italy.

This orderly became a star turn at the Colonel's parties singing 'Lili Marlene' in German, backed by the Colonel and Geoffrey. It had been the most popular song in the Western Desert, where all three had served. In fact it was also played frequently in the POW camp, the intention being to annoy the prisoners, but they actually enjoyed it.

This new Commanding Officer gave young Mike, our eldest son aged seven, permission to do PT every morning with the recruits and line boys of the

Assam Rifles, mostly Indian-born Gurkhas. Mike has since, many years later, been the Colonel in command of a battalion of the 10th Gurkha Rifles.

My move to Sadiya came early in 1945 and it was wonderful to be able to live as a family again, something five year old Robin had barely experienced. I do not believe Geoffrey had been able to be with us for more than odd months at a time. It was a great life for both boys. I taught them every weekday morning, with help from the Parents' Union School in England, who sent me out books and a syllabus and even examination papers for the boys to complete and send back. At weekends we would be out in the jungles around, where little streams ran out of the mountains to join the great Brahmaputra; swimming and fishing and cooking up our food on fires made from the abundant wood lying around. I regret to say VE day passed unnoticed but when VJ day came in August that year we celebrated with relief more than jubilance. Hiroshima and Nagasaki seemed right after the atrocities perpetrated by the Japs. We were just glad to know it was all over. Later a British doctor who had been a prisoner with the Japanese joined our community and we learned of the atrocities at first hand. Planter friends I met later had also been set to work on Death Railway, just surviving the treatment.

Meanwhile our life was undisturbed, with Geoffrey dividing his time between tours in the Mishmi hills and his work in Sadiya. The former meant we could all drive out in a 15cwt for the first twenty miles into the foothills where there was a small bungalow in which we could spend the night. Next morning Geoffrey would set off with men of the Political porter corps, carrying everything needed for many days. Wood would have been sent ahead, and the Mishmi people would be expecting the visit. The boys and I would return home, while Geoffrey would visit one village after another on foot. He would listen to any grievances and adjudicate in local squabbles. These were mostly about such things as A not having paid B the right amount of goats for his wife, or perhaps a complaint that either the woman or the animals were barren. Taking basic medical supplies Geoffrey would treat petty ailments, doing his best to get more serious cases carried down to the plains and a doctor. At the start everything needed was carried for the tour by the porter corps and I could neither send nor receive news unless there was anything urgent, when messages would be carried on foot. These tours could last a month or more. Later on, as light aircraft came to be used, more frequent supplies could be dropped by parachute. Items such as fresh bread were very acceptable and I could send mail.

Work on the plains was mainly administration and Geoffrey had First Class Magistrate's powers. Some of the cases he had to deal with were unusual, such as that of a man who came to him confessing he had killed another. He had had to do this because the latter had cast spells, first on his cattle which had died as a result. Now he was threatening his wife and so had to be killed, what else could be done? The case upset Geoffrey very much as he had to pronounce the man guilty, but had him sent to a higher court with the recommendation for mercy.

96

Another part of his duties was to attend local auctions at which Indian traders were permitted to be present to buy the goods brought in by the Mishmis and Abors. Normally no-one could enter the Sadiya Frontier Tract, as it was called, without a pass. Certain traders were given these and Geoffrey, or the Political Officer himself, was present to see the tribal people were treated fairly. One of the most prized articles for sale was musk, a gland from the musk deer, used in making scent. The musk deer was a source of food for the tribal people, also providing skins. These and the musk gland would be sold for salt, badly needed by these hill people.

Another essential item for them was opium, which they produced but did not misuse. It was kept for use medicinally, or to help keep them going in the most difficult situations, their life not being an easy one. In order to carry enough for use when travelling the Mishmi would impregnate a piece of cloth with watered opium. When needed a small scrap of the cloth would be cut off and soaked in whatever drink was handy and so imbibed. Geoffrey did occasionally do just the same after an exhausting day of climbing steep hills in appalling weather to reach some particular village he was due to visit.

Having learned Assamese, the language used locally and for Government work, there was also a need for interpreters, the *kotikis*, who translated it into the many local dialects. These were honoured positions and they were given red coats of beautiful English broadcloth to wear. These red coats were also given to the headmen of every village. This custom came about when the first government troops, wearing red coats, crossed into the Abor territory, resulting in what was later known as the Abor Expedition. When peace was reached the decision was made that red coats would be a sign of honouring a dignitary and they were worn with pride.

It was also an Assistant Political Officer's duty to help villagers who came for aid. On one occasion Geoffrey was asked to shoot a rogue elephant, doing immense damage and endangering lives at a nearby village. There were many herds of wild elephants in the jungles around and sometimes a bull elephant would be turned out of a herd. Whether it was an outcast because of its bad nature or only because there were too many bulls, it certainly seemed to enjoy creating havoc, and these were known as rogues. They would trample down the flimsy houses made of bamboos and thatch and destroy the granaries, that were merely huge, mud-coated baskets supported by bamboo poles.

Needing to have a look at the lie of the land before going out at night after this particular elephant, Geoffrey took me and the two little boys out to the distressed village during the day. The rogue only attacked it at night. At dusk he set out by himself to spend the night. Young Michael was furious at not being taken as well which, as the eldest son, though not quite seven, he felt was his right. Next morning when *ayah* went to get the boys up Mike was missing and no-one had seen him. After everyone had hunted everywhere possible I wondered if he

97

could possibly have tried to follow Geoffrey, who had taken our only transport, so I walked to Johnnie's and explained my trouble. He immediately set off with me in his Jeep. We had gone about five miles when we saw a small figure trudging down the road ahead of us. Although tired, Mike was not pleased at being taken home. He had missed nothing, the rogue had not turned up, presumably having moved to pastures new and Geoffrey had spent a boring and uncomfortable night.

Attached to the complement of Sadiya was the Political elephant which was called Joan, my name, which I found very annoying as I was teased by being told it was difficult to tell us apart from behind. All the same the trips we did on Joan at various times were most enjoyable; she was the most friendly creature.

Our bungalow in Sadiya was very close to the banks of the Brahmaputra river, the Political Officer's and the office were further away. When there were some particularly bad floods during the monsoon, Geoffrey was away all day rescuing people from low-lying areas and Joan was used to rescue families from their roof tops. While he was doing this the river rose higher and higher. Geoffrey had left me a small boat moored nearby for escape if need be. The rain continued to pour down and the river went on rising. I could see that the boat would be swept away unless I acted. Out I sallied at intervals to pull the boat further and further up the bank as the river rose. I got tired of getting my dress wet so in the end I took to going out in a bathing suit and tennis shoes, holding an umbrella over my head. I am glad there was no one there to take photographs!

Fortunately there was no need to use the boat as, just when I was organising our escape by it, the river stopped rising and the rain died down. We were very lucky because if we had got caught in the fast river current we might have ended in the Bay of Bengal, if we had survived at all.

22
Domestic Life, Sadiya

A new Political Officer was assigned to Sadiya, with a wife and two children, a boy and girl about the same age as our two. Mornings in both families were taken up with lessons. Like us they had a syllabus and books sent from Britain and we were all strict about the work being done. The four children had a lot of fun together but did get into trouble sometimes. Robin excelled at this on one occasion. General Wavell was Viceroy of India then and paid Sadiya a flying visit, literally. A small air strip, which we had not had, was prepared hurriedly for this important visitor. For the occasion it was surrounded by men of the Assam Rifles to keep it clear from the populace who were most excited at the idea of seeing an aeroplane so close.

The Political Officer, his wife, the Colonel of the Assam Rifles, Geoffrey and myself were all dressed up, standing ready to greet this VIP. The plane touched down and came to a halt. The Political Officer advanced as the door opened but, before he could get to the steps, out from the watching crowd appeared Robin, aged six. Making straight to the steps he held out his hand to Lord Wavell, who shook it, then brushed past him and disappeared into the plane. Poor Lord Wavell, not sure if this was a planned greeting or not, stood there uncertainly till Brian, the Political Officer, got to him and officialdom took over.

I was appalled and furious with *ayah* until she explained. She had brought both boys to see this exciting event, standing in the crowd with everybody else, but Robin had escaped through the cordon. The Assam Rifleman on duty did not stop him but refused to let *ayah* through to catch him; she was powerless. Almost worse was to follow. While we were lunching in the Political Officer's garden we realised that the British flag flying on the official flagpole was at half mast. A sign of mourning was not the right thing when entertaining the Viceroy, practically a rude gesture. This dreadful deed had been done by the four children. Both fathers were apologising hard but I do not suppose Lord Wavell thought anything of it, he must have understood. However both mothers were spoken to most severely for not looking after their children properly. They in turn chastised the children, who were not allowed to see the plane take off and were also given ten days 'CB' (not Confined to Barracks, as in the Army, but to Bungalow). This was a hard punishment as it meant no outings to the jungle streams, where they could swim in the clear waters, climb trees and enjoy themselves.

Another plea for help against a rogue elephant, probably the same one as before but in a more distant area, came and again Geoffrey was asked to deal with this. It was too far away to reach and return in a day so we all piled into a lorry, complete with tents, bedding and food, and set off for the village in trouble. As distinct from this rogue, the village had an elephant of its own; Joan had been sent there as well to make up a team to hunt the wild elephant down. On getting there we found the village sited beside one of the bigger streams, with dense forest behind it from which the rogue had come and disappeared again. We decided to pitch camp on the side we had arrived on, not wanting to have to carry everything across the water. As soon as they saw us the people used every available boat to visit us. A good camp fire was got going as plenty of driftwood was lying by the river.

The village elders gathered round to discuss the next day's operation and early next morning Geoffrey set out with both elephants, their *mahouts* and the best trackers from the village to follow up the rogue's trail. The boys and I were to stay in camp much to the formers' indignation.

By late afternoon, when no word had come since Geoffrey and his party had been swallowed up by the thick jungle early that morning, I did begin to worry. Darkness falls early and fast in India. As we waited it seemed a good idea to build up the fire. The boys enjoyed collecting logs from along the river bank. By the time it was really dark we had a big, blazing bonfire going. There was still no sign of anyone's return and there was nothing we could do except pile on more and more wood to make a beacon. This was the best thing to have done, because the glow of the fire in the sky did guide them back.

The jungle was so thick that they had lost the trail. On casting around in all directions to find it again, they had lost themselves. It was only the blaze that had guided them back. All agreed that the rogue had moved far away and was continuing his wanderings - we never again heard of him. I think Geoffrey was glad he had never had to shoot - he had not wanted to do that - but it was a job he was meant to carry out.

We had a holiday trip later on with elephants as Geoffrey was given a few days off duty. It was well-known locally that what was described as an ancient copper-domed temple had existed in a certain area that had been ravaged by floods long since. No-one had seen it for decades, but knew it had existed. Geoffrey asked if we could look for it as the area was not too far away, or so he was told. There was a young Raja who was very anxious this temple should be found and wanted to come with us. He had two elephants and we had Joan.

The elephants were sent ahead to where we thought would be a good jumping-off spot from the road and we drove out to join them. We had enough provisions for four days - all the time Geoffrey had been given. Everything was piled on to the three elephants and, tied in a basket behind the pad of the elephant, on which the Raja rode, were two pigeons. These were for a sacrifice to the gods when we found the temple.

First we travelled through tall, thick elephant grass; very slow and tough going, and we were forced to deviate slightly from our planned course. Once we got out of that we came to an area that plainly had been devastated at some time. Obviously there had been a total collapse of a hillside from a range we could see in the distance. This had brought down much soil, burying all in its way. Some giant trees still stood at intervals sticking up like skeletons out of banks of sand, the latter having been deposited on top of everything during the many monsoons that had passed since.

A lot of new growth had got established; young trees growing by little rivulets that had made their way in more recent seasons. Animal life abounded including big herds of various deer such as the sambar and the barking deer. We were able to walk quite close to them as they were not used to people and so were not frightened. It was a fascinating and never to be forgotten scene.

It was obvious that the copper temple was buried at some depth under all this debris and probably near to the hills from where the landslide had originated. No metal detectors existed then, or if they did we did not have one, so there was nothing we could do except enjoy what we had seen. We did keep looking hopefully for as long as we could but our time was running out - we had to give up. On our last night the Raja killed his two pigeons and we had them for supper. We had accomplished nothing but had enjoyed ourselves immensely.

23
Sadiya
1946-1947

Not many miles from us in Sadiya an American beaming station had been established to guide planes flying over the mountains to North Burma. These aircraft carried supplies to the Chinese army, then our allies against the Japanese invaders of Burma. This flight was known as 'flying the Hump', perilous because there were no maps at all of this mountainous, uncharted and barely populated region. These planes would take off from Chabua or other airfields in Assam and pick up the beam as a direction-finder to Sadiya. Once overhead there they would circle, round and round, mostly it seemed over our bungalow, mainly at night, until they located the new beam that would steer them over the Hump to their destination.

Sadly many lost the beam, navigation was too difficult and they crashed into these unknown mountains. Word was sent about missing flights to the Political Officer. He would inform his Assistant POs, Peter and Geoffrey, who would get messages out to the tribals in the Mishmi and Abor Hills. Lost aircraft were located but never with living crews.

When possible Geoffrey would travel to sites, bury the crew, retrieve identity discs and any personal belongings, which were sent to the American Headquarters. When the war was over an American War Graves contingent came to Sadiya and, with Geoffrey's help, located and disinterred the bodies, taking them home for burial in the States.

The personnel at the beaming station were very kind to us, inviting us to the movies when they had them. We were invited to supper and our sons had their first taste of jam on Spam and also wonderful American goodies such as delicious ice cream, chocolate drinks and Hershey bars.

When they were packing up and bound Stateside we were asked if we needed anything. This was near to Christmas 1945 and no sugar had been delivered locally. I had not been able to make a Christmas cake or pudding and asked if we could have some, if it was to spare. A few days later a truck turned up and deposited not only a huge sack of sugar but big tins of ice cream powder, fruit, Spam (for which they apologised diffidently), also the chocolate drink the boys had liked so much, amongst much else. We had a real feast that Christmas. There was some illicit wheeling and dealing in jeeps. A few were sold legitimately to the Political Officers for the frontier tracts. Many more good jeeps were driven into the jungle and hidden while write-offs were taken back to camp to keep numbers right. We were offered a good jeep privately but did not snap up this doubtful bargain.

1946 passed uneventfully for us, with my father spending the cold weather with us and the hot in the hills at Shillong. We paid him short visits to get a break from the heat, which was how we once got cut off from returning to Sadiya as planned.

The monsoon rain had been unexpectedly torrential and the road back was flooded and impassable. Geoffrey was due back on duty by a certain date and it seemed impossible until we remembered the river steamer service. Luckily this was due to call in at Gauhati just then, having navigated from Calcutta up the Brahmaputra on its way up river to Dibrugarh. From there we could make our way home.

Geoffrey, the two small boys and I managed to catch the steamer at Gauhati, abandoning our vehicle with its driver to follow when the roads were again open. The vessel was a shallow-bottomed, paddle-propelled boat; an ugly craft but perfectly designed for its purpose, which was chiefly to carry goods, but also passengers, up a fast-flowing river that continually changed its bed. My younger son has since described it as looking like a whale. He climbed on to its roof, which was a gently curved structure over the whole ship, and watched the paddles churning away. It must have been impressive as he was only six then.

We cabin passengers had a small upper deck to ourselves. The others all lived, slept and fed themselves on the lower deck, wherever they found a space. The cargo was the more important; mainly requirements for the tea estates, with tea being carried on the return trip.

We spent two nights on board in small cabins and because, unusual for the Sahib-log, we had no servants with us, I had to do all our cooking on an iron stove that seemed to be part of the engine room. No food was provided and we had to buy all our provisions before boarding and again when we called in at Tezpur, a town I was to know well in later years. For washing-up a bucket was let down over the side.

It was an unusual trip as no-one knew exactly which channel to take on a river that was twice as wide as normal, with a bottom of shifting sand. A lascar, an Indian seaman, stood sounding the depth continuously, chanting his findings day and night. We stuck on one sandbank; boats were lowered which towed us off. A boat was again lowered when there was a cry of 'man overboard'. Someone had seen what looked like a man's head floating past. The paddles stopped turning and we drifted downstream only to discover a football.

Great tree trunks floated past and other debris from the flooded land upstream. It was miraculous how the Captain manoeuvred that small paddle steamer upstream against the full force of a great river in spate. We reached our destination, Dibrugarh, on time, but our car did not get there for some days. I made a bad start to 1947 by breaking a bone in my spine, diving in the river, and needed to go to hospital. This was not easy as it meant crossing the Brahmaputra by a ferry made of two wooden dug-outs, with a deck of planks lashed together.

From this a motor car engine was attached to drive a propeller. Two vehicles could be driven onto the deck and on this contraption all the goods needed for the area were brought across.

After that it was a forty mile drive to the Civil Hospital in Dibrugarh. There I was put into a plastic jacket from my armpits to my thighs. Imagine my feelings on realising a few weeks later that I was pregnant. Our local doctor, an ex-prisoner of war of the Japanese, was not sympathetic. He merely said he would cut me out when I needed more space.

My baby was due in September and it was agreed I could not possibly leave it to the last moment to cross on the unreliable ferry, which often broke down, and when the river might be too high to be navigable. Shillong had the best hospital so my father came to my rescue, renting a house to which I and the boys made our way in good time.

24

Margherita - 1947

(Independence Day flag-lowering)

Soon after we had left for Shillong Geoffrey received orders that he was to take over as Political Officer in another frontier area bordering on Burma. He had to make this move from Sadiya on his own but with our most helpful servants. Nothing was broken or stolen, unlike some moves with professionals! The new Territory HQ was at Margherita, surrounded by tea gardens and was said to have been named by a lovelorn planter of old. On its west, divided from us by only a small river, was Assam's main oil field at Digboi.

After passing through tea estates to the east, the new area belonged to tribal people who were far better dressed than the more primitive folk of the Mishmi and Abor hills; and they wove beautifully patterned cloth. During the war a road had been constructed from Margherita to the Burma border known as the Stillwell Road, after the US General in charge. Running the length of the territory it left India at the outpost known as Hell's Gate. There was no Political Officer's bungalow, but the tea estate rented a *chung* bungalow, one built on stilts, for our use. On both sides of the road, after leaving the tea gardens, were the jungle areas of the tribal people. Thus we had modern civilisation on one side and old traditional tribal customs on the other. Touring in this Frontier Tract was not such hard work; it was not so mountainous and much of the travelling was done by dug-out, up and down small streams. For someone who enjoyed fishing as much as Geoffrey this was a pleasant change.

His first most important duty in his new district was on 15 August 1947 when, as the District Officer in charge, it was his task to lower the British flag and raise that of India on Independence Day. After that ceremony he drove out to Hell's Gate on the Indo/Burma border and did the same at that outpost. I still have the flag furled then which is, I am certain, the last British Union flag to have flown in India; it was lowered after other flags and on India's most eastern frontier. Years later I watched the film 'Gandhi' and the Ceremony of the Flags was portrayed as in Delhi. They used the wrong flag - an ordinary Union flag was shown but the British India flag has the Star of India in its centre as I can show anybody who would like to see it. When Geoffrey died in 1988 this flag was draped over his coffin at the funeral.

While he was busy with new duties, including touring an unknown Tract, I was a lady-in-waiting in Shillong. Just before my baby was due I went down with 'flu' and was admitted early to hospital. My baby graciously waited until I was over that and had one day out of bed before she decided to arrive on

27 September 1947, one month after Indian Independence, which was later to have implications.

Our old friend Johnnie, now in charge of all the Eastern Frontier Tracts, was able to send word to Geoffrey that he had a daughter. Early in November Geoffrey had leave to come to Shillong and at Carol's christening, Johnnie was godfather. No-one can have had a better one than he and I am happy to say I am still in touch with him and Mary, his wife.

When leaving Shillong in November for Margherita, Geoffrey drove the two boys by jeep, stopping for one night *en route* at a small *dak* bungalow, an official rest house. Baby Carol and I went by train a few days later, which took only the one day, being met that evening by Geoffrey in the jeep. Unfortunately a rather hot day in the train followed by a cold night drive in an open vehicle was too much for a six week old baby; Carol went down with pneumonia.

As soon as we realised she was ill we sent for the District doctor but he was away. Carol became too weak even to suck and we were desperate. Then we remembered the Americans had left some medical packages with us for use where they might be wanted. Geoffrey opened these and found the parts of a drip feed. Most of that night was spent by me expressing small quantities at a time of my milk into the glass container while Geoffrey regulated the flow through the tubing drop by drop into the baby's mouth. In this way we kept her alive until the doctor was found and could get to us.

25

Margherita - 1948

(sale of American surplus stores)

Now that the war with Japan was over the Americans, who had been working on the Stillwell Road, were packing up for their return to the States. The road they had built ran through the north-east corner of Assam up to the Burma border and onwards through Burmese territory, taking vehicles, weapons and aid generally to the Chinese, then our allies. It started on the plains, passing tea gardens, on through thick jungles, winding its way through dense undergrowth and climbing mountainous areas until it reached the Pass, called Hell's Gate and on into Burma. Geoffrey's district ended at Hell's Gate.

An enormous quantity of heavy machinery of all kinds had been needed to complete this mammoth task; not to mention all that was required for the men on the job. The Americans offered all this to the British Government, who considered the asking price too high. They also thought it would not be worth the cost of taking so much away to the States so the Americans would have to leave it behind - why pay for what you can get free? This infuriated the US authorities and they threatened to blow up, burn or bulldoze everything. The British Government agreed to pay but did well out of the deal, getting everything from bulldozers down to radios.

Wealthy merchants from all over India converged on Margherita to bid for all this equipment, items unobtainable normally in India. All this diverse material lay inside the Frontier Tract of which Geoffrey was in charge, and no-one might enter it without a pass from him. He was offered bribes by these rich contractors to let them through and bar their competitors. He might have done well financially, but this was not his way. Instead, not only did he issue passes to all on legitimate business, but did everything he could to assist, such as organising the labourers needed to move the heavy loads. As a Government servant he could not accept presents of money or valuables and gave his help freely.

It had always been considered correct for what was known as *Dhalies*, which consisted usually of baskets of fruit, nuts and sweetmeats with an occasional 'bottle', to be given at Christmas as a thanks for help given in the past year. That Christmas we were inundated, not only with the usual baskets but with Christmas cakes, puddings and chocolates from all the best caterers of Calcutta, chiefly champagne and other alcoholic drinks and numerous toys for the children. All this was considered acceptable, certainly by our servants who did well out of all the fruit, etc, and by our boys who had never had such goodies before.

These were all gifts as a thank you for the help Geoffrey had given. The givers had left with all they wanted and needed nothing more from Geoffrey; they need not have thought of him again. We had a very cheerful Christmas, able to entertain our friends with champagne, but we kept one bottle for a special occasion. The trouble was that we could never decide when an occasion was extra special.

We were due for 'repatriation' from India so we kept it for our last night in Assam, then thought Bombay would be a better place to drink it, but instead took it on board the ship home. On arrival in England it was finally opened when we reached the home of Geoffrey's parents. It had gone flat!

Since we were unable to remain on in the rented bungalow after Christmas because it was needed for a rejoining tea assistant now freed from his war service, we had to find other quarters. Thus 1948 began with a hunt for accommodation and the only empty buildings we could find were the remains of a temporary military hospital, put up hurriedly in the emergency of war. This consisted of two parallel hutments, long and narrow, that had been wards. It did have a few doors and windows down its length, but nothing more.

We decided it could be turned into reasonable housing with one ward for ourselves and the other for kitchens and servants' quarters. It stood beside the small river at Dihong that separated us from Digboi, Assam Oil Company's HQ with its oil wells and 'nodding donkeys'.

We set to work with a piece of chalk, marking out on the concrete floor where we would have the walls to divide it into rooms and where the doors should be. A place for a fireplace, in what was to be our sitting room, was indicated by a chalk circle in one corner. I drew a pleasant design for a brick fireplace.

Unfortunately we had to leave the area for a few days so were unable to oversee the work. When we got back we learned it was all complete and we could move into our new home. Work had gone well except for one thing, which gave us a horrid shock. The attractive fireplace I had designed was not what I had pictured. My rough chalk circle on the floor had been used as the shape needed, not merely as a guide for positioning. We were faced with an erection that looked like a cross between a Hindu temple and a beehive, with tiers of brick curving up into the corner of the room up to the ceiling. An eyesore we had to live with, but worse for me was the thought that future occupants would believe it was my design.

No water was laid on but a pipe was sunk between the two buildings. After a few days there, the entire household, including servants, were cursed with runny tums. No water closets of course so the poor sweeper was overworked. Cook was blamed for not keeping the kitchen hygienic and everything was boiled, scrubbed and disinfected to no avail.

A sample of the pump water was sent to the chemists at Digboi, who reported that we had struck oil but not in a sufficient quantity to make drilling worthwhile. We had been drinking something like diluted liquid paraffin, as used medically. Once our water problem was solved we were quite comfortable, with electricity laid on.

The boys became ten and eight years in that January 1948 and very active. They rigged up a nightline across the river alongside and with a small dugout attended regularly to baiting and collecting the fish caught; and very tasty they were. They also went with Geoffrey on his tours of his territory, visiting villages, mostly by dugout. They were even able to see an elephant *kheddah* in operation. A stockade was built with one entrance with a funnel-shaped fencing path leading to it down which the wild elephants were driven and so captured. I have never understood how wise animals like elephants could help to drive their wild kin into captivity.

May drew nearer, the month we were to leave India, now independent. Since 15 August 1947 Geoffrey had been working for the Indian Government, now we were due repatriation with no idea of what would happen to us once we reached Britain. Neither Geoffrey nor I had been to England for twelve years and the children had all been born in India. My father, who had been living with us, returned to the Shillong hotel to wait and see what would happen to us. It was certainly time for the boys to go to a real school, though I had done my best to teach them as regularly as life allowed and as far as I was able.

We sailed on *SS Franconia* from Bombay after some difficulties to get on board. Vaccination certificates were demanded by the port officials, who were happy to accept the forms for Geoffrey, myself and the two boys because there were Government stamps on them, although these had been done by a tribal area vaccinator, an almost illiterate Naga. Carol had been vaccinated by the highly-qualified doctor at the hospital where she had been born eight months earlier, with the scar visible. The doctor had provided a signed certificate but it had no Government approval on it. The port officials were adamant; this would not do, she could not travel. Geoffrey did not waste time arguing. He shepherded us out of sight of the authorities, rummaged through his suitcase and produced the signet he had been using as a Political Officer. He borrowed an inking pad from a nearby office and made a slightly smeared but official looking mark on Carol's certificate.

We waited a while and then tried again. This time the port officials let us pass quite happily as there was now an official looking stamp to be seen. We were allowed to leave India, wondering if we would ever return.

26

Balipara Frontier Tracts

1949-1952

Our ship, *SS Franconia*, was overcrowded; full of expatriate families like ourselves and Anglo-Indians, as well as troops. We were split up; I was given a good cabin with a bathroom, but shared it with three other women, two small boys and two babies, including Robin and Carol. Geoffrey was down in the depths with several other officers, while Mike was with about six other boys and an ex-schoolmaster.

There were so many babies on board that getting nappies dried became almost impossible in the limited space given us. No Pampers or any throw-away nappies then! Eventually we mums took to tying them onto the railings round the deck and the ship became festooned in nappies. This continued until another ship passed ours and sent what we heard was a rude and ribald signal to our captain. After that lines were rigged up on the Well deck and we were able to hang our nappies there.

Arriving at last on a Sunday morning in Liverpool we were more than a little upset to be told we could not leave the ship because it was a Sunday and the dockers were not working. As a result our baggage could not be unloaded and we could not leave the ship without it, but we were not allowed ashore at all. Many relatives of those on board had come long distances to meet them. Geoffrey's elderly father had come all the way from Sussex. Neither he nor any of the other relatives and friends of the passengers were allowed on board. We spent that Sunday waving and shouting to those standing on the dock. There were a number of soldiers on board who had been fighting the Japanese and were at long last home again after years away. Their wives and children stood there below and had to stay there. We did not get off the ship till nearly midday on Monday. It was not a very cheering return to England, having been there last in 1936, twelve years ago.

Ration cards, points for certain foodstuffs and coupons for clothes and sweets were heaped upon us. Geoffrey's mother was quite overcome to receive five more ration books and so many points, exclaiming that she did not know how to spend them. When I suggested a tin of peaches, something we had not seen for years, she was appalled, 'My dear, they are twenty points!' Although we all needed clothes for the English weather and had plenty of points, we were short of cash. I regret to say we sold some coupons so that we were able to use the cash on ourselves. Soon Geoffrey was job-hunting, finding being a District Officer and dealing with primitive tribes was not much of a testimonial. Neither did having fought both Germans and Japanese help; there were too many returning soldiers better qualified than him. We were lucky in having a home with his parents. Then, most unexpectedly, came a letter from the Government of India asking Geoffrey if he would like to return to his post as a Political Officer in the Frontier Tracts. Gratefully and gladly Geoffrey accepted and before long was on his way back to India.

Before he left he saw to it that the boys had their first seaside holiday, tasting the joys of investigating rock pools as the tide ebbed, digging in sand, and building castles to defend against the incoming waves. I would have liked to return to India with my husband but we both felt our sons could not be left to face a new life, including boarding school, without one of us there. From then on my life became one of either leaving my children behind and joining my husband, or leaving him to spend time with them.

My in-laws were very good to me, and I could at least visit my sons and take them out, be there on Speech Day and for Sports Day. Then they were home for their first Christmas holidays. It snowed, which was a novelty, and the trees looked so beautiful, coated with frost. I remained in England until after the next summer holidays. My father, feeling lonely in India, made the trip to join us, taking the three children and me to stay in a hotel in Paignton, so Carol too was able to play on the beach with the boys. After taking them back to school, my father, Carol and I boarded the P & O liner for Bombay. I did not enjoy leaving my sons but my husband had been left all alone for a year.

At Bombay there was the usual train journey to Calcutta, but things had changed. Geoffrey met us there and said we were booked to fly from Calcutta to Tezpur in Assam and were not going on by train - a few hours instead of a night's travel. This was the first of many flights in Dakotas all over India.

Geoffrey's posting in the service of the Indian government was to a new area. He was now the Political Officer of the Balipara Frontier Tract, under the authority of the North East Frontier Agency, NEFA for short.

He was now on the western border of NEFA territory, an area extending northwards to Tibet, with tea gardens to the south stretching to the north bank of the Brahmaputra River. Through this land ran the Borelli river, one of the biggest tributaries of the Brahmaputra and a river that came to mean a great deal to us.

Carol and I arrived at the beginning of the cold weather of 1949 to join Geoffrey and remained there until 1952. I had liked our life at Sadiya and at Margherita but neither place had been exactly full of social activity. Now, living with a number of tea gardens not far off, things were different. There was a Planters' club at Thakurbari, with tennis courts, a golf course, a small swimming pool and films every Saturday night. Also there were frequent parties both for the children and adults. Most of the planters' wives had Khasi *ayahs* like our Nadybon, who had rejoined us, and had lots of company since the children and their *ayahs* always went where their parents did. Pleasant as the Club was, it was not the most pleasurable feature of our lives; this was the Borelli river. Some of the best times of our lives were spent either on it or by it, even in it!

As I have said, the Balipara Frontier Tract stretched along the Tibetan border - a buffer between it and Assam's plains. Numerous streams, big and small, flowed out from the Himalayan range to join the Brahmaputra. The biggest and nearest to us was the Borelli, pouring out from the mountains behind, its waters racing through rocky gorges, roaring on over great boulders until it reached the lower slope where the more tropical jungle took over. Flowing on more gently through thick undergrowth on its banks, tumbling over shallow rapids until it split into separate runs, each monsoon causing some changes of course. Some banks were covered with thick jungle to the water's edge, others formed sand banks. Some channels wound their way through areas of thatching grass, on until the runs united and it became one big river again, wide as the Thames, continuing gently past tea plantations and rice fields until it joined the Brahmaputra.

A track had been made, parallel to the Borelli, running up to the gorge, there it left the foothills to a place called Bhalukpong. A 'pong' is a salt lick, where animals of all kinds would gather. Bhaluk was the king of that area in ancient times. He was said to have had a palace there but we never found a trace of it bar a few chiselled stones.

From a ridge high above the water we could look down a long length of this beautiful river - an unforgettable sight. This road never stood up to the power of the monsoon rains and had to be opened up at the beginning of the cold weather.

In the hills above lived the Daflas, primitive animists, clad only in loin cloths but with intricate helmets of woven bamboo with a peak in front. They had long hair tied into buns under this peak and topped that with the beak of a hornbill, all held in place by a bamboo skewer. When it rained they would collect one of the giant leaves from the trees around or a wild banana leaf and pin this on their heads. On their backs they carried a shoulder bag made of closely woven cane, a vicious plant that was abundant, its thorns catching and scratching the unwary passer-by.

Daflas (note their curious headgear)

27
Geoffrey on Tour

During the rule of the British Raj it had been the policy not to interfere with the hill tribes and their way of life. They were allowed to carry on in their old traditional life style with minimal intrusion, merely a paternal eye cast their way to see all was well.

That meant that the people of the deep interior never met anyone beyond their own village, except their next door neighbours on each side. Anyone further away was considered an enemy. Those who traded, like the Sherdukpens, would often visit the plains and those who lived near, and in, the foothills such as the Akas and the plains Daflas would visit local plains bazaars. There were others who had never seen or met any but their neighbours, no plains Indian, let alone a white man, had ever visited them.

Geoffrey with two Daflas

The Indian government chose to try a new policy. The whole of the country was India and they were proud of it. This unknown territory was part of India and should be administered as the rest; it was to be opened up to 'civilisation'. Geoffrey was ordered to visit these uncharted areas and explain to their people that the new government wanted to give them roads, hospitals and schools; things they knew nothing about, just as they knew nothing about a change of government. They were to be made full citizens of India - not an easy task when those concerned had no idea what that meant. A strange thing was that the first Indian government official they met was an Englishman and an old Etonian.

Complete with a platoon of Assam Rifles, the force that was half-police and half-soldier, for border security, armed with a machine gun, a two-way radio and its generator, Geoffrey set off on his mission. Everything for this tour into the unknown had to be carried by porters as usual and, of course, extra porters were needed to carry the food and goods of the original porters; it was always a problem in logistics.

Inspecting the Assam Rifles

Passing first through familiar country with friendly village people was no problem, with interpreters to translate the Assamese that Geoffrey spoke into the local language. As they progressed, more interpreters were needed to translate obscure dialects to the first interpreters, until there was quite a string of interpreters interpreting to interpreters.

On reaching the distant villages they were attacked with bows and poisoned arrows and also blow pipes, by villagers thinking an enemy was raiding. Having no wish to hurt these innocent people, Geoffrey withdrew and then ordered the machine gun to be set up. The Riflemen did this and were ordered to aim at an outstanding clump of big bamboos. Firing a long burst back and forth across the whole clump, the bamboos were fast toppling down under the eyes of the scared tribesmen. Geoffrey had no further trouble with the over-awed people. As he progressed through the area he used to provide evening entertainment by working the generator in the dark. This gave forth a fine display of sparks to the unsophisticated audiences. News travelled ahead and he was welcomed. This is not to say there were no more difficulties; anyone who has journeyed in jungle terrain knows that.

To my mind leeches are the nastiest. I have plenty of experience of knowing how they could scent one from afar, drop off a leaf onto the back of one's neck and crawl into every crevice of the human body. There is little to be done to keep them off; we always carried little packets of salt, as a sprinkle of that caused them to shrivel up. If you tried to pull them off they left a wound that hurt for days. Smokers had an advantage as a glowing cigarette end did the trick, but neither of us smoked. Jungle cane was also devilish, seeming to reach out and catch the passer-by with the sharpest of thorns, like teeth, up the spine of every leaf. Virulent nettles - the sissini from which the Akas wove cloth after boiling it, grew in unexpected spots. Innocent-looking trees could cause stinging for days if brushed against.

On top of all this grew the tall elephant apple tree, whose botanical name I do not know, but be careful all who walk beneath its laden boughs. Without warning its large, heavy fruit could drop like a bomb and knock you out if it fell on your head. It was a necessity to learn what to look out for and yet that same jungle could be so beautiful: wild orchids, pink, yellow and mauve, festooned branches; tree ferns spread their delicate foliage under vast trees.

In spite of these hold-ups the trip was successful to the extent that the whole area to be visited was seen and roughly mapped, with the party returning in good order.

During his absence Carol and I carried on our carefree social life, and for me this meant bridge! I had played even in my school days during holidays spent with relatives. Recently bridge had not figured often, but now there were morning bridge parties with planters' wives and even on some evenings at the club. Sadly Geoffrey would not and could not play. While a prisoner of war the others had tried to teach him, but failed - he preferred to tunnel.

For some reason Carol, taken to her first Christmas party, got hysterical at the sight of the Father Christmas. There were many of these parties in various bungalows and she had to be removed, screaming, from every one. Only the biggest party at the club remained to be attended; I was desperate. As I sat reading aloud 'The Night Before Christmas' to Carol, prior to next day's party, Geoffrey returned home.

He had been visiting the Miris and they had given him a baby deer they had found, whose mother had probably been killed by a tiger. We did wonder though if it could have been the Miris themselves, not seeing the baby until too late. Coming into the room he called out to Carol to come and see what he had got. When I suggested that perhaps it belonged to Father Christmas and had got lost, she accepted this with enthusiasm. We made up a feeding bottle, and the little deer took this hungrily from Carol. Not very originally we called it Bambi, from the story book.

Next day when we went to the club Christmas party she marched straight up to the Father Christmas of that day as soon as he appeared and told him not

116

to worry as she had found his lost deer. As it was very small she would look after it for him. Luckily one of the young assistant planters who was acting the part played up very well. Fathers were always found out by their children and were never chosen.

Bambi grew into a fine buck and we had not the space for him, but were scared to let him loose into a jungle life he did not know. Luckily we heard of someone who had a female, and passed him on. The pair were being given to a zoo but during transport there was an accident. Bambi broke his leg and had to be shot - a sad end, but he had had a pleasant life.

Carol and Bambi

117

28

Visits from VIPs

Many important Indian government officials visited us at Balipara, including the Governor of Assam. I had to be exceedingly careful when laying on a lunch party for him, as he was a very strict vegetarian, not eating even eggs or onions.

Because he came to inspect the District, entirely new to him, coming as he did from Delhi, all the head men and elders of the many hill tribes were called into headquarters to meet him. They gathered round in a great half circle; in front of each group stood the *kotikis*, the interpreters, resplendent in their red coats, as were the headmen of each village. It was a colourful sight with so many people of different tribes, ways and dress.

The Daflas with their odd helmets, the Cikas in cane crowns, the Sherdukpens well adorned in jewellery and the Miris in their special red handwoven sarongs. The Governor stood at the open arms of the semi-circle, Geoffrey, Nari Rustomjee, head of NEFA, other officials and myself around him, and addressed them. There was total silence while he spoke in Hindi as none of them could understand a word. Then Geoffrey, the Englishman, translated for the Indians in Assamese. This was partially understood but soon all the many *kotikis* were translating the speech into their various dialects. It was like Babel.

A popular hill sport was then demonstrated, requiring a youth to shin up to the top of a tall, slender tree. Once up he would tie the end of a long rope of split bamboos, which he had carried up with him to the top. On his way down he would strip off the branches with his *dao*, or knife. The top of the tree was then dragged down to about eight feet from the ground and tethered to a bamboo stake, making it into an arc. The game was to leap up and catch the trunk and then, by a series of bouncing movements, move higher and higher up the trunk. The winner was the one who got highest. This was 'Climbing the Bobo'. Both Geoffrey and Nari (ex ICS and Bedford College) tried this but got nowhere, the winner getting at least three times further than they did.

Another VIP to visit us was Sir Archibald Nye, the British High Commissioner to India, and Lady Nye, during a round of the British community in Assam. Being there on behalf of the British government they stayed with the most senior British tea planter. As both were keen fishermen, Geoffrey was asked to lay on a day on the Borelli for them, taking them out in a rubber dinghy as was the custom. Collecting Sorai to help paddle, Geoffrey took the Nyes with him. I followed behind in a borrowed boat with two other Miris and the *Aide-de-Camp*.

Geoffrey, as the Political Officer, interpreting the speech made in Hindi by the Governor of Assam, Sri Prakasa, to representatives of the hill tribes; Joan in the background

Geoffrey in a group including the Governor of Assam, Sri Prakasa in centre and Nari Rustomjee, Head of North-Eastern Frontier Agency (NEFA)

Lady Nye fishing in the Borelli river with
Sir Archibald in the background

Luckily the fish took well that day and Geoffrey was told by the Nyes that they had never had a better day's fishing. Returning by jeeps at dusk after an enjoyable day out, the leading vehicle with Geoffrey driving the Nyes, met a leopard on the track. As the beast leapt back to avoid being hit, it almost fell into my lap as I sat in the front of the second vehicle. Twisting away it shot back into jungle edging the road and disappeared. Who had the biggest fright, I or the leopard?

The Daflas did little or no cultivation but had herds, among which were moufflon, a cross between yaks from Tibet and plains buffaloes. Each year they would visit the plains to trade and obtain much-needed salt. Geoffrey would commission them to open up the road until passable for jeeps and lorries, and to cut tracks off the road to chosen spots on the river bank. These were for access to the water, places where one could picnic or camp and launch our boats, carried up on the roofs of jeeps.

121

It was this accessibility to the river that gave us such enjoyment. Like many of the planters we acquired a rubber dinghy, an ex-RAF or USAAF life boat. By carrying these inflatables to whichever spot we chose we could launch them and float down the river with the minimum of paddling. Our driver would take the jeep to a given landing-spot. It was possible to fly fish from the boat, casting into the bank as we floated down river, then stopping off at likely spots, here and there, to do some spinning, have picnics and swim. On the fly it was a fish called the *boka* we caught; when spinning, usually the *mahseer*, a fighting fish. Both were eatable but bony.

Another tribe under Geoffrey's jurisdiction was the Miris, a river people, living on the lower reaches of the river, whose boats were their livelihood. These were dugouts, and when a new one was needed they would come to Geoffrey for permission to cut down a suitable tree. As the District Officer his agreement was needed. Then the village headman and others would look for the right shape and size of tree, as near to the river bank as possible. This was important because after it had been felled and hollowed out with only hand tools, it had to be dragged to the water's edge to launch.

The type of dug-out used by the Miris on the Borelli river;
Sorai, the Headman, with a gun

122

As you can imagine they were expert boatmen and we used to employ Sorai, the headman, and a good friend of ours, and his brother to paddle our dinghy so that we could get more fishing. We always gave them a fair share of our catch, usually a good one as the Miris knew where the fish might lie.

Every cold weather we would have built a hut, called a *basha*, made of bamboos and thatch, with the help of the Miris, and spend every weekend we could camped by the river. Every monsoon it would be washed away and we would rebuild. Wild animals abounded; you could be sure of seeing something - a sambar or a barking deer, the chikor, a tiger or leopard, possible a herd of elephants, a boar and monkeys galore, swinging their way through the treetops. Even little turtles basking on a log by the water's edge, who would fall in with a splash when surprised. Plenty of bird life as well; hornbills being the most exotic, with their great curved double beaks, so prized by the Daflas for their headgear. So you can imagine visits to our hut were taken whenever possible and we did not skimp on comfort. As we used to say, 'Any fool can be uncomfortable' and we were not fools.

Geoffrey with a friend in his 'basha' on Borelli river

A couple of servants usually came with us; this was considered by them to be a treat. We provided their food while out, and there was fish or other game to augment the basic. Sorai and one of his mates would always come and it was a standing joke that they would not get 'hooda baht' or only rice to eat. Also a tot of rum was given him as we all sat around a roaring camp fire in the evening deciding on what route we should take next day.

We were always welcomed when we paid a visit to Sorai's home and would sit outside his house, having been given rice wine or rice beer of his brewing to drink, by his wife. We never went into the house, a thatch and bamboo longhouse on wooden stilts, as this was not the custom.

Wife of Sorai, the Headman, weaving a red sarong

Once, when we learned that his wife was very ill and in great pain in childbirth, we hurried to one of the tea garden doctors, a great friend of ours, for advice. George insisted on returning with us and saved the life of mother and baby. He was the only outsider ever allowed in a Miri house. The people of Sorai's village were Hindus, though not at all strict, but they were strong and healthy with numerous offspring.

Just across the track that separated the two villages was another, also of Miris, but Christians. They had come under the influence of American Missionaries, very good folk who ran a hospital. Unfortunately they disapproved of alcohol and told their converts that to drink it was a terrible sin and they would go to hell. These Miris came to Geoffrey in great distress; their women hardly ever conceived and when they did the babies died or were sickly. This was a serious matter.

'What are we to do?' they asked.

There was only one difference between the two villages sited so close together, one drank their home-brewed rice wine or beer, the other did not. Geoffrey realised that they needed the nutrient of the alcohol as part of their diet and told them so. The result was that he had the missionaries' fury vented on him for leading these good people into eternal damnation. There was dissension in the village but the Christians were winning the argument. The last we saw of them their numbers were still diminishing, while Sorai's villagers continued to flourish.

124

Headmen from the Sherdukpens on an official visit

29

More Tours

(among the tribals, Miris & Daflas)

Geoffrey had to do a great deal of touring, most of which was to the west of the Borelli, where lived other tribes. One of these was the Sherdukpens living in the higher hills, whose territory stretched up to Tibet, with whom they did much trading. Much of their wealth was hung around their women's necks in the form of jewellery studded with turquoise and lapis lazuli. It was through their lands that the Dalai Lama fled from Tibet some years later.

Touring was again all on foot, with porters, and Geoffrey would be away for a month or more. The Sherdukpens were friendly and hospitable, welcoming him as he approached their villages, with a big bowl of their local brew, and did the same when he left. To have refused would have been insulting but he sometimes visited several villages a day and found he was becoming unsteady before finishing his visits.

Because he had to accept each drink, the only thing to do was to cut down on the amounts offered, so he had his own special bowl made of walnut with a silver lining, but quite small. He would whip this out of his pocket before a large bowl could be handed to him - this was acceptable.

Living high in the mountains their clothes were thick and made of wool from yaks. In the foothills lower down the slopes, were the Akas, more primitive and in less need of warm clothes. On their heads they wore a sort of crown made of a circlet of bamboo. Their women's faces were painted with black spots - who are we to laugh at that, thinking of lipstick and the black patches once fashionable?

More Daflas lived to the east of the Borelli, but could be approached more easily by the only bridge over it, well downstream. This motorable road led past many tea gardens before reaching a smaller river, the Bordekir, up whose reaches Geoffrey would travel on foot.

So by these various routes he would visit many of the tribes, but not all; others were tucked away in areas he never visited.

An Aka man wearing their usual bamboo hat

An Aka woman carrying her wealth around her neck

30

Geoffrey Changes Job

(Indian Tea Association - Dibrugarh)

Home leave was given only after three years, so it was the summer of 1951 before Geoffrey had a chance to see Mike and Robin again. We did all have a wonderful holiday together, driving an ancient Austin Countryman to the Costa Brava. This was before it became so popular, and Tossa de Mar, where we stayed, was a quiet, delightful town with uncrowded beaches. We swam and took up snorkelling, the new craze then, with Carol, not even five years, diving to depths far below the rest of us.

In England it was the year Mike had to move on from preparatory to public school, so we were most thankful Geoffrey could be there for the beginning of Mike's first term if nothing else. This was a dreadful period when I kept being in the agonising position of either leaving my husband for my sons or vice versa, never able to be with both except for the briefest of times. Much as Geoffrey enjoyed working for the Indian government in such interesting employment, he had begun to worry about the future and the lack of security, with no pension due. Therefore when, half way through 1952, he was offered a position with the Indian Tea Association, he accepted and sent in his resignation from Indian government employment.

Naturally he could not leave Balipara immediately, and it so happened that India's first Prime Minister, Pandit Nehru, and his daughter, Mrs Indira Gandhi, came on tour to Assam while we were still there. They visited us at our bungalow and Pandit Nehru asked Geoffrey if he had enjoyed his work.

'Very much', he replied.

'Then why are you leaving it?' he was asked.

'I have no future or pension,' he said.

'I would easily see you got both' Pandit told him. 'You could become an Indian citizen and be put on the permanent cadre and get a pension.' There was a pause. He went on, 'I am prepared, here and now, to offer you Indian citizenship.'

I held my breath, wondering what Geoffrey could say, knowing he would not want to give up British citizenship, nor wish to offend.

'My father would not allow me to do that,' he said, 'but I greatly appreciate your offer.'

Indians do, or did then, take filial obedience very seriously, so Pandit Nehru said no more, accepting Geoffrey's decision. All the same, schooled and at University in England as he had been, he must have known this was an excuse. He and Mrs Gandhi shook hands with us and left. I was impressed by them both.

I, too, had enjoyed life at Balipara but it had become a bit galling. We had tea planters living close by, being, as we were, on the border between the tea gardens and the foothills of the tribal area. They had well-furnished bungalows with all the conveniences of electricity and water laid on. We still had oil lamps and the old 'thunder boxes'. To go to a party only a few miles away and spend an evening with 'all mod cons' and come home to oil lamps, and sleeping on the veranda to keep cool got irritating. It was pleasant to think that we would soon be living under those same agreeable conditions when we moved. It did not work out quite like that.

Geoffrey joined the Assam Branch of the Indian Tea Association, known as ABITA, and was posted to Dibrugarh, Assam's major town. The ITA was formed by several tea companies combining, like a Union, with their officials, secretaries and advisers, assisting tea planters in various difficulties: trouble with labour; hold-ups in supplies such as coal or oil, and generally assist in the smooth running of all those tea company estates which belonged.

The Assam Branch was divided into two zones and Geoffrey was an assistant secretary to Zone 1, under the branch secretary. We had been told we would have a new bungalow but when we got there, discovered we were to stay with the branch secretary, who did not really have the accommodation for us and Carol for a long stay. On asking on arrival about our new bungalow, we were told it was not yet built! In fact the first thing we did was to locate the field a couple of miles out of Dibrugarh town. That land had been given by a local tea garden, but we had to mark out boundaries for a bungalow for ourselves and one for a new chaplain, due soon.

We had no instruments other than a measuring tape and plenty of pegs and string. With these we did succeed in marking out boundaries for two bungalows needed. It was not easy; the field was very rough, with long grass, and we needed all the geometry we had learned at school, especially Pythagoras' Theorem to get right angles in the corners of the plots. Months later when we flew in a light plane over the site, we saw that one of our right angles was not a right angle at all in any sense of the word. Watching our bungalow growing, and laying out our garden was entertaining for a while but it got tiresome not to have a home of our own.

Our first host, though very kind, needed his spare rooms and we moved to a bachelor planter's bungalow. His servants were not used to a memsahib in the house, and I objected to their methods of hygiene.

With Christmas drawing closer we felt we had got to be in our own house by then. It was ready apart from door and window frames so we decided not to worry about them and moved in. It was enough to have electricity, water laid on, both hot and cold, and loos that flushed - real luxury. Everything was better for us; extra pay, a pension and more leave. There was a good hospital, which was lucky as Carol needed a tonsil operation very soon after our arrival there.

Geoffrey was not a tea planter but an officer of the Indian Tea Association, which included most of the big tea companies such as Brooke Bond, who owned numerous estates in Assam and elsewhere. He had a variety of tasks, some of them mundane, such as seeing the processed tea was shipped by river steamer or taken by train with no hold-ups. More exciting were occasions when the labour force was incited into violence against the managers. Geoffrey did rescue planters who were being attacked. Being fluent in Assamese and Hindi, both spoken by the labour, he was able to calm down rioters sufficiently to get negotiations going.

Luckily we were in an area which had telephones, so it was possible to get news quickly, but there were still places where the only way was for a light plane to drop messages. Several of the bigger gardens had their own planes, such as Cessnas with ex-Forces pilots who combined flying with tea planting. Some of the most senior tea planters around us were real old die-hards. They did not expect to go to the ITA office when advice was wanted or do anything other than what they had always done. Geoffrey was told he must always be at the club on club nights so they could consult him there. This made going to the club work, not relaxation or entertainment.

To get to our bungalow from the main road we drove down a track on which was sited a weighing point with a thatched roof, for newly plucked tea. With this track now in more use it was causing hold-ups when weighing was in process, so the whole thing was moved. A very senior manager exploded in fury at this because it was under this roof he always had a sleep on his way home from the club on Saturday nights. It was he who insisted that Geoffrey should always be at the club.

Camping and fishing on Borelli river

132

31

To Tezpur - 1954

(on local leave - fishing)

After several months working for the tea industry Geoffrey was given a month's local leave, and we were invited to stay with planter friends of ours working from our old haunts. When we had been at Balipara, David and Peggy Gibbs were on a tea garden not far away and the four of us often went fishing together.

Plans were made that we should have more of these pleasant trips on the Borelli river again with them. Getting there on the Saturday we were told that there was to be a gymkhana at the Polo Club the next day. Peggy had been pushed into helping with the lunch and I said I would accompany her. David and Geoffrey decided to go fishing. If I had known what was to happen I would have gone with them; instead I went with Peggy.

The gymkhana was mainly for mounted events, held on the polo field, but there was one race in which ladies, astride men's bicycles, were to hit a polo ball along a course with polo sticks. I did not want to enter, but was urged on by Peggy, she being much too short to reach the pedals. Foolishly I agreed. Not having cycled for years I was not any good at steering up the course. When I found myself heading straight for the tea tables I leapt down from the saddle, forgetting it was a man's cycle, and not having noticed it had a 3-speed wire running about an inch above the cross bar. I landed on that. The wire cut through like a cheese cutter and I saw blood running down my legs. I ran into the polo pavilion followed by Peggy, who had seen what had happened.

Making for the changing room that had been prepared for ladies to use, I found only a 'thunder box' and an enamel bowl of water on a table, a small towel and a pile of the red jackets polo players wear. None of this was suitable to staunch my bleeding. There was no first aid box or any medical supplies, which I had expected to find in a polo pavilion. Apparently there never was, because the regular doctor was one of the players and kept everything in his car. Unfortunately he was on home leave and his locum had not attended the gymkhana. He was sent for and when he came I was put into his car and taken to the nearest tea garden's medical post; it could hardly be called a hospital, although it did have what might be described as a theatre.

I was laid on the operating table and found I was facing a line of clear curtainless windows, beyond which was a veranda. Soon word got about that a memsahib was the emergency patient, and what seemed to be the entire labour force of that estate lined up, peering through the glass at what was happening. I was the star of a theatre performance. It was useless to complain and the sooner

I could get stitched up the better. Peggy had come with me and seen it all. As she told me later, she was hoping I had not realised what an audience I had drawn.

With Peggy, David and Geoffrey all off to the camp site that David had fixed up, early the next morning, I was stuck on a limb. There was no way that I could go with them as planned. The locum doctor was exceedingly kind and took me back to his bungalow where he and his wife took wonderful care of me. I had lost a lot of blood and the doctor wondered about a transfusion but I would have had so far to go to get this he decided, rightly, to leave me in peace. I was not up to returning with Geoffrey at the end of the week but was able to fly back by Indian Airlines later.

Soon afterwards the Indian Tea Association decided that, with only two zones in Assam, a third was needed to cover the area in depth. Zone 1 Headquarters was centred on Dibrugarh, Zone 2 on Jorhat, further down river, but both were on the south bank of the Brahmaputra river. Zone 3 was to be near Tezpur, close by the Indian Airlines airfield. It was also near our old HQ at Balipara on the north bank.

By now Geoffrey was considered experienced enough to take on this new district, one with which he was partially familiar. We were delighted as, once again, we had the Borelli river not too far away. Also we had many planter friends there, not to mention our special Miri pals: Sorai, his family and the villagers, who were all equally pleased to see us.

Although back to the same type of house, built on stilts, known as a *chung* bungalow (though not really a bungalow), amenities were very different. This was tea garden property with a brick office in the same compound and we had electricity and water laid on. It belonged to the Sonabheel Tea Estate and was merely rented.

Another bonus was that Carol was able to join some other small children, all being taught by one of the two doctor's wives, together with her own daughter Gilli, who became Carol's best friend.

Geoffrey even got permission from the new Political Officer to build huts (*bashas*) on the river bank as before, and was able to get aid from his Miri friends. He was also again appointed honorary Forest officer for the north bank jungles. Being near the IAC airfield was also a help, not only for its daily service but because the light planes from tea gardens landed there. There were times, especially in the monsoon, when roads would be cut by flooding, then Geoffrey could have a Cessna or other light aircraft sent for him.

Once when Geoffrey was wanted, the Manager invited Carol and me to visit, as he too had a small daughter. We were to go for one night only but there was such a downpour that night, with the heavy rain continuing all next day, that the Cessna could not take off from the flooded grass strip. A commercial Dakota, which delivered cold storage of all kinds on a monthly basis to several estates with such strips, was due in the next day, but it had been cancelled that day. We were feeling most unwanted guests, asked for one night and had already been there three. We felt we were eating up all available food especially when the expected cold storage did not arrive. On asking our host if there was no way we could leave, Geoffrey was told of one possibility. There was a tea garden some miles away which was not badly waterlogged and where the cold storage plane was to try and land on their airstrip. It was all a bit uncertain but we took the chance.

First we were taken by Land Rover to where the river between this and the next tea garden was normally easily fordable. Now there was so much water, not even a Land Rover could cross. The only way over was to wade, with the water up to our waists. Geoffrey carried Carol and two of the garden labour force took our suitcases over on their heads. The manager of the estate on the other bank had been alerted and came to meet us in a lorry. We climbed into the back in our dripping clothes and he took us back to his bungalow, where we were able to change into dry clothes from our suitcases. We were then taken to the air strip in time to meet the incoming plane. It landed with a great skid on the sodden grass and I did not feel too keen on embarking. A mass of goods of all kinds were unloaded. There were assurances on all sides that it would now be easier to take off and we climbed aboard. All went well and we landed with no difficulties on the regular Indian Airlines airfield at Dibrugarh. From there we were able to catch the normal air service back to Tezpur, the airfield so near our bungalow.

New employment brought new terms, including more frequent leave - four months every two years - but we still did not have the advantages, as became more common, of having school children flown out in their holidays.

My father had now taken to living permanently with us, instead of only in the cold weather. As he pointed out, the elderly prefer to be warm, so he would rather remain for the hot season. He gave us the best of treats by having both boys flown out for the Christmas holidays and we all enjoyed Christmas dinner in our *basha* on the riverside.

Among the victuals taken out with us was a dingy, bedraggled-looking live duck, bought by cook in the bazaar. This was a form of emergency rations; we always hoped to catch enough fish to feed everybody, or possibly shoot some jungle *murghi*, the ancestor of the domestic chicken, but it was wise to have something in reserve. The drab duck soon made its way to the river and after a few swims, lo and behold, it became lily white, though not quite a swan.

Early each morning we would gather round the camp fire, soon rekindled into a blaze, and have a 'cuppa'. The duck took to joining us and when offered tea in a saucer it scooped it up and this became a routine. Luckily there had been no need to fall back on reserves; in any case it had become impossible to look upon it as anything but a pet. It returned home with us, remaining a pet known as Lily.

Another pet with river connections was Arthur J Rankop, *rankop* being the Assamese for 'turtle'. Poor Arthur J was not looking too well so Mike decided to examine him by opening his mouth, the only part possible to look into. Arthur J shut his mouth tightly on Mike's finger and would not let go for some minutes. We decided Arthur J would be happier back on the river bank. Mike still has the scar to this day.

My father, a keen fisherman, used to go fishing regularly even though he was nearly eighty. He would board one of the Miri dugouts, with three of the men of the village as crew. They would paddle upstream and he would trawl a long line behind the boat. This was impossible coming downstream as the current was too fast, so he was landed on likely banks to do some spinning. He had good catches both ways. He celebrated his eightieth birthday by catching a fine fish and we gave a dinner party for him that evening at which he was able to tell everyone about it.

The Miris became somewhat worried about a year later, feeling the responsibility of taking so old a man out, on such a fast and deep river in an easily up-turnable craft, was too much. They explained their fears to Geoffrey, afraid that they would be blamed if there was an accident. My father was told, and begged his crew to carry on; it gave him so much pleasure. He and Geoffrey promised faithfully that, whatever happened, the Miris would never be blamed, and their word was accepted. So my father carried on until he was eighty-two realising then that enough was enough.

Joan's father with his crew and the fish he caught on his 80th birthday

136

32
Schooling Dilemmas & Chinese Invasion
1957-1962

By 1957 we realised it was time for Carol to start a proper education, which meant boarding school in England. Mike had left school and was at Sandhurst Military Academy, but Robin still had nearly two years to do. We found a prep school not far from him, which helped when visiting them both.

After three years of this we rebelled against orthodox views of children being sent to Britain and brought Carol out to India. It still had to be a boarding school, as there was nowhere suitable near us, so she went to Hebron School that was mainly for missionaries' daughters, with the equivalent boys' school nearby. Carol was able to come home for holidays - a long one during the cold weather and a short break in the heat, as the school was in the hills of Coonoor in the Nilgiris. This was a pleasant, peaceful period for us and we enjoyed having our daughter for holidays. She now tells me it was a very poor education, short on languages and science but she is a superb grammarian and a top class speller! 1962 was a year I will not forget, so full of tragic events. We were on home leave and my father had gone to the hotel at Shillong. We had taken a flat in South Kensington; Robin and Carol were both with us, Mike being in Malaya. We'd even arranged French lessons for Carol. She and Geoffrey, both addicts of Nureyev and Fontaine, spending much time outside the stage door! Our happiness was shattered by a phone call from the doctor of the Welsh Mission Hospital in Shillong to tell us that my father had had to have major surgery and blood transfusions but was now out of danger, though he must remain a bed patient. Our leave was nearly over so he told us to finish it as there was nothing we could do to help.

As soon as we got to Calcutta, Geoffrey returned to work at Tezpur, Carol to school at Coonoor, while I made my way to my father in Shillong. I found that his one hope was to be able to return to our bungalow and be with us. This looked almost impossible as he needed so much nursing. His faithful bearer, Daroga, who had been with him for nearly fifty years, had died a few years earlier but he had taken on a new servant, Abdul Gani, who turned out to be a treasure. During the entire time, until my father's death in hospital after about five months, he had slept every night on the floor by his bed, scarcely leaving his side until I arrived to take my turn. It is quite normal in hospitals in India for relatives to stay by the bedside of patients, even feeding them.

Luckily for me my father had taken his car and driver to Shillong, so I was mobile, and I had a very good friend, Cynthia, with whom I stayed. It was less than a month later that dark clouds appeared on India's north-east frontier. The Chinese had already taken possession of Tibet and it looked as if that had not contented them. They made demands on Indian border territory. The rumblings during September grew to action by October. Indian troops were moved to meet the onslaught.

The Nabobs of the tea industry began to worry about their interests on the north bank of the Brahmaputra. Visitors of varying grades of importance, from London and Calcutta, descended upon Geoffrey. I felt I should be there to support him in coping with these visitations; my father was no better, or worse, and though he enjoyed my company I could not really help him. Having his car to use I began a shuttle service between my husband and my father, each journey taking a full day.

Geoffrey had been appointed liaison officer between the Indian General's HQ nearby and the tea industry. He had to keep in touch daily and the reports he received were not good. The Chinese were advancing steadily, wave upon wave of Chinese soldiers, like a flood. As one line of men fell those behind picked up their weapons and advanced until they fell and those behind them carried on in a never ending stream. It caused a loss of morale; that as much as anything else, defeated the Indian soldiers. This continued until 20 November. It was a Sunday and Geoffrey and I decided to have a day off fishing on the Borelli river. We did well and returned to the bungalow in the evening in a cheerful state of mind. Geoffrey felt he should make his daily call on the Military, not expecting it to be urgent. It was most urgent! He was told the Chinese had by-passed the Indian troops and were in the foothills about twenty-five miles away from us. If we had chosen another area for our day out we might have met them.

He was given orders that all foreigners, i.e. British, on the tea gardens must be evacuated immediately and he was to see to it. There were no phones and the area was a strip about 300 miles long, so messages by hand must be sent to all. I shall not forget that evening; I sat at my small typewriter, typing out explanatory messages as fast as I could. A Muslim friend, Micky, from Calcutta, was staying with us. He and Geoffrey worked out the best way to spread them over the district, Micky going one way and Geoffrey the other and getting those on the nearest estates to take a bundle of messages and pass them on and so spread out the message-bearing like a fan.

The first person Geoffrey called on was the manager of Sonabheel, the estate on which we lived. It was nearly midnight by then and Mike, the manager, was driving up to his bungalow when Geoffrey arrived. He could not believe this was not a trick as he was just returning from a party at the Indian Air Force Officers' Mess and there everything was as usual; they seemed to know nothing of events. I did my message delivery, too, because I had remembered that a married couple near us was off early next morning by car to collect a daughter from school in Shillong for the Christmas holidays. They were leaving their two younger children with their *ayah*. All was in darkness when I got to their bungalow, they having gone to bed early because of the early start next morning. The sound of my shoes (Indian servants go barefoot), as I walked down the long veranda at midnight to their bedroom door, woke Tricia up. She told me afterwards it was a sound she would always remember. Anyway I was able to rouse them and they set off at once, taking the younger children and *ayah* with them. Motoring back home afterwards I felt very thankful that I had remembered them in time.

Our messages told everyone to rally at our bungalow as soon as possible as we were nearest to the airfield. Only those in the furthest area to the west were to motor direct to the airfield at Gauhati, as being nearer to them and to Calcutta.

The first families arrived about 3am, their husbands returning to their tea gardens to ensure all would be left as well, when they themselves must leave. The flow continued and by midday there were about seventy women and children gathered under our roof, most of them hungry. Luckily tea was no problem. Another bit of luck was that, expecting Carol home for the school holidays, I had ordered and received a food parcel from the Army & Navy Stores in London. This contained several packets of biscuits, a tin of Klim (a milk powder), several packets of Kellogg's cereals and packets of Knorr soup powders amongst other things. We had expected to camp over Christmas and had laid in stocks for that.

We were able to dish out tea and biscuits to the adults and delicious cereals to the children. When midday came I got Cook to tip all the varied soup powders in one big *degchi* producing enough soup for everyone. Bread was easy as Cook made ours on the spot and had just done a big bake up. So all were reasonably fed.

At last, soon after the meal, Geoffrey arrived with cars to take the first consignment to the airfield, and the women with the youngest children went off. It took three loads before the last of us were taken: my special friends, Barbara and Merle who had no children, and a couple like me whose children were at school in Britain. Suddenly I realised I had got to leave everything behind just as the others had already done. Up till then I had been so busy that I had not given a thought to how it affected me. Now it hit me hard.

Knowing I too must now leave, I went round the bungalow unlocking my storeroom, the drinks cabinet and the linen cupboard. I called the servants together and told them I now had to leave but would prefer they took what they wanted rather than let the Chinese have it. Thanking them for all their help I handed out all the cash I had in the house, which was not much as we worked on the 'chit' system, signing notes.

Picking up the small suitcase I had packed, not knowing what to pick, and not allowed more than one could carry, I joined my friends Barbara and Merle. As we were driven out of our gateway tears were running down my cheeks, not for what I had left behind, but for whom.

At the airfield we were ordered onto an Indian Air Force troop carrier that had just brought in reinforcements. Only the wives of planters embarked as their husbands had returned to their estates to leave them in as good order as possible; except for one couple with crates of Scotch as their luggage. He was later given early retirement for leaving so early.

We were flown to Gauhati, next airfield on the route to Calcutta, from which there were regular flights by Indian Airlines Corporation to Calcutta. Amid chaos IAC were doing their best to get both the British wives from the tea estates and panic-stricken Indian families, terrified at the news of the Chinese invasion, away to Calcutta on whatever available Dakotas were arriving from there.

Having no child to think of I was content to wait my turn, especially as I was not sure what I should do. A few hours drive from Gauhati was Shillong where my father was lying in hospital. On the other hand my daughter was due to arrive in Calcutta within a week, from school for the Christmas holidays. I had intended going there anyway in a few days time and decided to do that and take advantage of a free trip!

Eventually I got a seat on a Dakota; the only Briton left among all the Indian families. On reaching Dum Dum, Calcutta's international airport, I found all the British wives who had already arrived had left the airport. I was the only one; this had me worried as I had no means of transport and no money, having given all I had away. There I stood in the bustle of the airport crowds, feeling so alone, no idea of what I should now do, when, to my amazement, from out of one of the doorways poured all the men from the tea gardens, who we had left behind, and amongst them was Geoffrey.

This was like a miracle. I had last seen him when he had left me with the IAF officers. He was then off to round up the planters themselves. He had told me he had no intention of leaving unless it became impossible to stay any longer; then he planned to launch our rubber dinghy onto the Brahmaputra river and paddle downstream. I had done all I could to help him by collecting things he would need: an oil hand lamp with oil and matches, bottles of drinking water, whisky, what food I thought best and blankets. To see him there, safe, was a great relief when I had not known when I would ever see him again.

Apparently the British High Commission in Calcutta had realised they had better do something to help the British community in this crisis. Up to now everything had been done by the Indian Army and Air Force and Indian Airlines, but now BOAC (the forerunner to BA) came onto the scene. They flew a plane direct to Tezpur; the airstrip was only just long enough for it to land and the planters were embarked. Geoffrey saw them on board and the doors were shut. He was walking away when IAF officers seized him and practically threw him on board into the cockpit of the BOAC plane, onto the laps of the crew. They flew straight from Tezpur to Dum Dum; a much more comfortable flight than their wives had had.

140

One thing had not been thought of when arranging this rescue and that was food. There was no pretty stewardess with her trolley on board. The men had been on the go since before dawn - it was now after dark - seeing that the factories and offices were left in as safe a position as possible. They had not thought of eating, but as they left their bungalows they had snatched up the bottle of Scotch they were saving for Christmas. Once on the plane the bottles were opened and consumed on empty stomachs. The result was that it was a very tipsy body of men who turned up at Dum Dum. A BOAC coach was standing by to take them all to BOAC's Calcutta office and I was able to go with them.

A reception committee of the British High Commission officials and the top brass of the tea industry was there to greet us with cups of tea. Somehow this seemed very funny to the merry passengers on the coach and there was a great burst of loud laughter as we drew up. It was at that moment I realised I was a refugee and I guessed the tired, hungry men with me did too. We were well looked after; the cup of tea was welcome to me and accommodation had been fixed up for everyone. We were quickly whisked away by our new hosts, Ted and Lynn, who we had once had visiting us officially. Both worked at the Bengal Chamber of Commerce, housing the ITA, and Ted had been transferred from the jute side to that of tea, and had been sent to us to see tea in production. Having heard we were keen fishermen they had brought their rods and learned more about fishing in Assam than about tea there.

Luckily Ted was Geoffrey's size, because the latter, not intending to leave when and how he did, had nothing but the clothes he stood up in and had been wearing them since before midnight. As we sat after a welcome dinner listening to the radio, we heard that the Chinese had informed the Indian government that they had advanced as far as they had intended. They had made a claim on the terrain bordering Tibet, which was now theirs, and having proved their point they would retire to the area they considered right. This meant that the land on which the tea gardens stood was no longer threatened. Geoffrey's first reaction to this news was that he must get back as soon as possible. Next morning he and Ted met up with the others in the tea industry. A plan was worked out whereby key personnel would be flown back the following day.

At dinner that evening, November 21, Geoffrey apologised to me for not giving me a single birthday present. Whereupon Ted and Lynn began to laugh and explained that it was also Ted's birthday, but they had not wanted to embarrass us. We then celebrated both birthdays. Although Geoffrey and Lynn have both died since, all four of us got together whenever we could. Even now Ted and I try to have lunch together on November 21, and usually manage it. Together with certain planters, such as the managers of the biggest estates, Geoffrey returned on November 23 by Indian Airlines to Tezpur. To his amazement our bungalow, which had been in a mess when I had left it on 20, after coping with so many families, was again in perfect order. Everything was clean and tidy and in its right place. Our servants appeared immediately and handed over the keys which I had left with them and not one thing had been taken. They could easily, and legitimately, have taken so much, such as our radio, silver, clothes etc. Not only that but our cat, chickens and ducks had all been fed. I have to admit not everyone was as lucky as we were.

33
Shillong Again
1963

Meanwhile I remained with Lynn in Calcutta, intending to await Carol's arrival from boarding school a few days later. I was not able to do this because I received a phone call from Cynthia in Shillong. She had kindly kept an eye on how my father was doing and told me he was sinking; I should come as soon as I could.

Naturally, after arranging with my friends Barbara and Merle, with whom I had left Tezpur, to meet and look after Carol, I left for Shillong. I found my father very weak, scarcely recognising me and muddling me up with my mother - dead so long ago. He kept asking when we could return to our bungalow. Thinking to cheer him up, I told him I was now here to stay with him, not continually leaving as before.

'I want to go home' he kept saying. Stupidly I told him even I could not go home at present; we were not allowed back and I would be remaining with him. Sadly this disappointment was too much for him. He died on 3 December, 1962, aged 87. He is buried in Shillong. Fishing was always his favourite pastime so I asked the Khasi priest if I might have carved the original Christian symbol of the fish on his headstone, and was allowed to do this. Khasis are devout Christians of many creeds.

Eight years later, when we left India for good, a dear Khasi friend of ours, Cyril, offered to look after my father's grave as if he was one of the family. Khasis always care for family graves. We were told by Cyril that on his death his daughter would look after both graves. Cyril has died since but I am sure his daughter will do as he asked.

It was early December when my father died and still the 'powers that be' would not let any wives return to Tezpur; most of the men had returned by now. The ITA office in Shillong had a small flat adjoining it, often let to planters on local leave. I was able to rent this. Contacting Barbara and Merle in Calcutta I found they had no wish to stay there and were happy to join me, bringing Carol with them.

We thought we would be there over Christmas but, to our joy, were allowed to return home on 23 December. Of course all the goodies I had ordered from the Army & Navy Stores for the holidays had been used up when feeding the families while we waited for our evacuation. All the same it was a better Christmas than we had expected, though tinged with sadness that my dear father was no longer with us.

Some understanding was reached between the Indian and Chinese governments about their joint frontier. The Chinese returned to Tibet. The Indian government continued with their policy of opening up what had once been Geoffrey's old district of the Balipara Frontier Tract.

Roads were built - no need now for touring on foot by the Political Officer. Small air strips were made. VIPs could visit easily. One visit caused some consternation. The radio message said to prepare for the MOH. The local officer in charge translated this to mean that the Minister of Health was paying a visit. The small hospital was scrubbed out; all the bricks and boundary stones were whitewashed. Everyone put on their best clothes to meet and to greet their guest. The plane landed, its doors opened and out poured a flock of goats. 'MOH' should have been read as 'Meat on Hoof'.

In the last days of Geoffrey's term as Political Officer he had depended to some extent on air-drops when on tour. I was once allowed to go on one of these air-dropping flights - something I will not forget. A commercial firm in Calcutta had taken on the business with light planes and Australian pilots. They ferried urgent machinery, spare parts and frozen food to the tea gardens. They also agreed to air drop supplies into the hills on free fall - no parachutes. I had no comprehension until then of what lay behind 'them there 'ills' I could see every day. The sheer, steep heights and depths were beyond my imagination. To fly over one mountain ridge, seemingly almost touching its tops and see the deep drop into the valley below was breathtaking. Then to be barely skimming the next peaks was quite an experience.

A dropping zone had been chosen in the least precipitous valley. Nearby villagers were warned to keep clear from the dropping zone to avoid death from the heavy packages hurtling out of the skies. Needless to say the people were far too curious to obey fully.

I remember well my Aussie pilot getting apoplectic at the sight of a group peering up just after a load had been pushed out. His language might have been worse if I had not been alongside.

After the invasion, the IAF took over what part of this was still needed - not much now that there were roads into the distant tracts. The IAF also patrolled both hills and plains, much to Carol's annoyance. She was unable to continue sunbathing in a secluded part of our garden because the IAF took to hovering over it.

We became good friends with our IAF neighbours; some even more RAF-like than the RAF, with their handlebar moustaches. Trevor became a special friend, a flight lieutenant who, like Geoffrey, was keen on duck shooting. Between them they hatched up an effective scheme.

There was a vast area of marshland, *bheels* as we in Assam called them. This was a favourite feeding ground for thousands of ducks, mainly teal but also pochard and mallard. Geoffrey often had to visit the tea gardens all around this *bheel*. When such a visit was due he would let Trevor know. He, in his turn, would wangle to do a helicopter patrol over the area. They would fix a

144

rendezvous and Trevor would hover over the part of the *bheel* he saw most populated by ducks. Geoffrey would see him and in his Land Rover would find a route to where Trevor was indicating, easy to see by the commotion among the birds. From the ground the high, thick grasses made it too difficult to find the right spot but were easy to make a way through once you knew where to go.

Next Sunday we would pick up Trevor and set out for the day and make for the place now located. A happy day was spent by all. We would take a picnic, mostly sandwiches, but often including Scotch eggs, a dish new to Trevor which he called 'Grenades' but enjoyed. Although a Muslim he didn't take food restrictions very seriously. Once he said he would bring the sandwiches and gave orders to the Mess staff. When he tasted them he was mortified and apologised profusely. They consisted only of bread and tinned butter; to his Mess, this was a sandwich.

If you think badly of us for shooting such lovely birds as ducks, please remember this was in the 1960s. Duck flew in from Russia in their millions at the beginning of winter to a pleasant climate and flew back in early spring for breeding. What we shot was a tiny proportion of all that came and they were never shot at on the water - that was unsportsmanlike! Also take note how appreciative the IAF boys were for this tasty addition to a dull menu. In fact they pooled up to buy cartridges for Trevor to use.

We, too, liked a change from goat, bazaar chickens and the occasional very tough piece of beef, killed surreptitiously; news of which would be passed round secretly. Cows were not generally permitted to be killed in India.

34
Home - House Hunting
1964-1965

By 1964 life had returned to normal. To us the Chinese invasion might never have happened; it seemed just an unpleasant and even an exciting interval, possibly a nightmare.

It was not long before life changed for us as a wealthy and childless aunt of Geoffrey's died and he was one of three nephews to benefit, giving us enough to afford to buy a house. Until now, when on home leave, we had looked at houses for sale but never had the wherewithal to do more than look. Now, at last, we could actually buy one! Geoffrey was due home leave that summer but, for various reasons, the India Tea Association could not spare him. However, hearing his mother was not well, he asked if he could have just one month instead of the usual four, which was agreed.

We were able to spend plenty of time with his mother, who, I am glad to say, recovered quickly, and yet we managed to find the house of our dreams. Geoffrey went back to work while I stayed on, completed the sale, spent one month in the house, got it well enough furnished to be able to get a tenant for the next six months and returned to India.

The following year, 1965, Geoffrey was able to take the balance of his leave. Carol was now over seventeen and it was time for her to study for a future job; it was also time for her to get a new passport. We applied to the British High Commission in Calcutta who issued what they claimed was a valid passport as a British subject.

Making our way to Dum Dum, Calcutta's international airport, to catch the KLM plane to Heathrow on a Saturday evening we were all very excited. Our first ever home of our own was waiting for us. Geoffrey had only seen it when viewing, and Carol not at all.

Imagine our horror when at the Customs and Immigration desks we were told that Geoffrey and I could go through but not Carol. Her passport was insufficient for her to leave India, as she had been born in India after Independence and Geoffrey and myself were Indian-born. Argument got us nowhere and it looked as if none of us could travel on the plane, now waiting impatiently on the tarmac. We asked to see a higher authority to be told that as it was Saturday night no-one else was available. Then someone had the bright idea that perhaps the girl was going to the Britain for further education.

'Yes,' we chorused.

'In that case it is permitted,' we were told. Thankfully we dashed out across the tarmac as fast as we could to the waiting aircraft, just as the steps were being removed. Inside the plane we got black looks for keeping everyone waiting so long. Carol now has another passport issued in Britain with the magic words 'British Citizen' in it. That makes all the difference but she has not, as yet, returned to India.

For us India had lost much of the hold it had upon us. We now had a home of our own, something I had never had before. No longer did we merely live in whatever building was allotted to us, making it a base but not minding where it was. Now we yearned for our own home.

Nor did the fact that I was ill a lot, as never before, help. I got bad bouts of amoebic dysentery. This resulted in my being sent to the Shillong Hospital for three weeks, every afternoon of which I had to spend having a retention enema. To those who have experienced the unpleasantness of ordinary enemas I leave it to their imagination what the retention variety is like. To those blessedly innocent, I will not give any descriptions.

I was also hospitalised with tropical bronchitis but only to a local hospital run by the kindest of American missionaries. It was while I was a patient there that our devout and abstemious Padre Wylde fell ill. He needed a blood transfusion and it was a Saturday night, so word was sent to the Club, knowing most planters' families would be there. Everyone immediately rushed to donate their blood, arriving around midnight as merry as they were keen to help. All the blood the padre needed was pumped into him; extra donors waited all night in case they were needed. He made a quick recovery, saying later he had never felt better. We were all sure it was because he had never had so much alcohol in his life.

We passed through 1964, 1965 and 1966 more or less uneventfully; some illness, including Geoffrey getting measles, for which he was teased, but found very useful as he could escape into the jungle, fishing or shooting and pleading the need to isolate himself.

Home leave came at regular intervals of two months each year, when we made our way to our precious house, redecorating at least one room each time. We also acquired the best dog in the world, from a young planter leaving to live in Australia where dogs from India are not allowed. Many wanted him but David picked us, chiefly because Geoffrey had learned that he was to go to Shillong which was cool in the hot weather. This dog, Whisky, was a Labrador, hating the heat and liked his new life, since Geoffrey, only acting for the present incumbent, spent the hotter months of '65 and '66 in the cool. Whisky was an amazing dog; he had Field Trial champions in his pedigree, but up to three years old had never heard a shot fired, his master having been keen on games, tennis and football. He was well-trained and a professional at getting goats out from among tea bushes.

Geoffrey wanted a gun dog and thought with time and care Whisky could be taught. It did not need any time at all; on his first outing to a *bheel* he knew exactly what to do, collecting up the fallen duck from land or water; it was in his blood. He gave us a scare once because he became the prey of a buffalo leech when we were shooting near a village not on our favourite marshland. Buffalo leeches are twice the size of a normal leech; hard to give an accurate length because they increase in size as they suck blood. We got the leech off but they inject something that stops blood clotting and the blood continued to pour out. Nothing we could do would stop it; poor Whisky was losing pints. Driving into the village nearby we were directed to the local doctor. He was appalled at the idea of treating a dog but when we pointed out that Whisky would die if nothing was done and it would be worth his while, he agreed to stitch up the wound. Vets were very rare people to find except in towns, which seems odd as animals are not generally town dwellers.

35
Last Years in Shillong
1967-1970

1967 brought the next change to our lives; Geoffrey being transferred to Shillong because James, for whom he had acted during leaves, was retiring to Britain. Having remained for twelve years in our Tezpur bungalow - the longest period in which we had ever stayed in one place - this was a horrid upheaval.

The move had advantages - extra pay and seniority. Geoffrey was now called an Advisor instead of a mere Zone Secretary. We would now live in a hill station, 5,000 feet above the plains, so no more torrid hot weather. Unfortunately after so many years in the heat we were used to it, disliking the cold much more. Also we did not want to leave people and a place of which we had become so fond.

Promotion meant dealing directly with the Governor of Assam and his ministers on behalf of the tea estates all over Assam. The bungalow and its garden were far grander than any until then. The house was furnished with large mock-Tudor pieces, a baronial-type dining table, chairs matching and heavy carved sideboards. Green lawns stretched around the house with tall trees, eucalyptus included, beyond. It was sited on the slopes of a high ridge over 500 feet above. This ridge lay to the south blocking out all sunlight from us until midday.

Inside the house it was cold and draughty, as it was built on stone pillars with badly-joined floorboards. When the wind blew the carpets billowed. Only three fireplaces, so the bedrooms were chilly and, because we were at the very end of the electricity line, hardly any heat came through. I have never before or since felt so cold indoors. Grandeur did not mean comfort - there was even a ghost! We learned that it was that of Noel Ward, the retired tea planter who had built the house and after many years died in it.

We did not believe the story until Ken and Patricia Rawson-Gardiner came to stay and she said she had seen a ghost. We laughed at her but when she pointed out a particular man in a group photograph adorning a passage wall, saying, 'That's the man I saw. I can recognise him easily,' we felt we should check. We sent for an old servant who had worked there for many years.

'Do you know the Sahib in that picture?' we asked.

He replied without hesitation, 'That is Ward Sahib. I worked for him here.'

Not only that convinced us, but when Patricia said she had seen him in the one small and cosy sitting room and Anthony, the servant, confirmed that it was Ward Sahib's study, there was no doubt. We lived there for three years and never saw him, nor did any other of our guests.

149

Every weekend we could, we tried to escape to the plains, or at least to one of the jungle areas lower down than Shillong. We became friends with some Khasis, especially Cyril, a retired Government officer, who knew well all the streams and valleys. With his know how and our equipment we made interesting sorties into delightful and secluded places off the beaten track, usually returning with a reasonable catch of fish or a brace of jungle cocks. Sometimes when there was a Government holiday we would camp beside one of these hill streams as they tumbled their way down over rocks on their way down to the plains.

Joan's catch of a 44lb mahseer, at Tezpur, 1962

150

One Christmas a niece Veronica Barton, working in Kuala Lumpur, was able to join us for her leave. For our Christmas holiday we had picked a place in the plains, not far off the road from Calcutta. A nice bit of light woodland, or *garchi*, beside a small river with good *bheels* alongside, teeming with wild duck. There we would have our Christmas camp. Veronica and I went ahead, taking the servants, plus tents, other equipment and supplies. The remaining five of our party were to join us in the evening after their working day was done. We felt we had done a perfect job; tents all pitched, cook and his camp kitchen ready for action, with the rest of our party due at any moment.

As we congratulated ourselves on our success, into one end of our encampment appeared a herd of water buffalo. They proceeded to trample their way, with no turning aside, from end to end of our camp. Nothing stopped them, not our yells and stick waving, not even our dog who did his best to turn them aside. Anything and everything in their way went under their hooves. At the peak of this chaos the rest of our party turned up. The buffalo continued on their way home regardless. We had chosen a site directly on their route to their village, taken each evening and they saw no reason to deviate.

We did not let this spoil our Christmas; somehow the camp was resurrected. We had an excellent Christmas dinner with wild duck instead of turkey, but still had the traditional plum pudding, boiled in a reconditioned kerosene tin over a wood fire. Our servants were also able to celebrate with wild duck added to their rice and lentils; all except cook himself - a vegetarian Buddhist.

About this time Geoffrey developed an irritating rash on his chest and saw a dermatologist on his next home leave who told him he was allergic to tea! This was most awkward, working as he did for the tea industry.

Part of his job was visiting Assam's Government ministers; to keep on good terms with them was essential. As soon as he entered a Minister's office it was a greeting to him, then a call to the *chaprassi* or orderly, 'Bring a cup of tea for Mr Allen.' Geoffrey then had to explain he was not allowed to drink tea. Very embarrassing, and he felt it weakened his position as ambassador for tea.

In the light of much later knowledge, which Geoffrey was never to know, I do not believe tea was to blame. It was too much sunshine; when on jungle or river expeditions he always cast off his shirt. Now we know that sunshine can cause cancer and it caused his death, even though it took twenty years or more for this to happen.

36
Farewell to India
1970

After working for three years in Shillong, the day came for Geoffrey to retire. Our many years in India were over; born in 1912 and 1913 respectively and having spent most of our lives there, it was now 1970 and time to leave the country.

There were still moments to treasure and painful ones as well. Leaving our servants was so sad; our Muslim bearer's wife fell on her knees with her arms round me weeping. There were tears on all sides.

Before we left the country we were invited back to stay in our old Tezpur bungalow with John and Mollie Tessier Yandell. John had taken over from Geoffrey. It was great to be back there; parties were laid on and, to our great delight, a day out on the Borelli river. Even the Indian government gave us a treat by fixing up a visit to the area that had been part of Geoffrey's old territory when Political Officer.

A car was provided to take us up to Bomdila in a morning, a trip that used to take Geoffrey many days on foot. Several of the old headmen and elders had gathered to meet us at what was now quite a town. A lunch was provided including yak tea, something I had not tasted before. I found it rather more soupy than teaish, due to the melted yak butter instead of plain milk. I felt that I must be polite and drink it up, so I drained my cup, only to find it quickly refilled. With a great effort I drank this and again in seconds it was full again. Luckily Geoffrey caught my eye and signalled to leave it undrunk. Afterwards I learned that if you finished a helping it meant you wanted more. I should have only drunk half of my first cup.

We also met the old office staff; the Head Clerk's wife had herself woven a lovely cloth, with a border of Indian women fishing with a special basket-like scoop, because she knew I enjoyed going fishing. The clerks also gave us a tall brass *paan* (betel nut wrapped in leaves) dish. They pointed out that it all came to pieces for easy packing but they had not thought of how heavy it was. All our luggage had gone ahead and we just had light cases for air travel! However we could not abandon a present that meant so much and ended up with it in our hand luggage.

All this made leaving much more heart-breaking; only the prospect of our own house awaiting us and to be able to have our family with us kept us going. After these pleasant interludes we flew to Calcutta, sad to be leaving Assam. From Calcutta we were flying on to Bombay, having decided to leave India by sea in the old traditional way. Before we left this busy city we felt we should really look at it. Our many previous visits never seemed to have taken us further than the hotels, clubs, such as the Tollygunge, shops and the Hogg Market and some burra sahibs' houses. Now we felt we could not leave without at least seeing a little more and became tourists for the one day we had left.

We were conducted to places like the Jain Temple, where all life is sacred and the priests sweep the ground before them as they walk for fear of killing even an ant; something we knew of but had not witnessed. The Victoria Memorial was a familiar sight but we had never been inside it before. Taken through back streets and areas of the city not known to us, it hit us more and more how little we knew and it was now too late.

In Bombay we stayed in the Sun 'n' Sand Hotel and could not resist a swim. We did get taken to the island on which were the Elephanta caves and its temple, held up out of the water by tall carved pillars and swarming with monkeys.

Then it was off to the docks and boarding our ship. Standing on the stern we saw the great archway, 'The Gateway of India', fading into the distance; in our hands we each held our topees, not worn for ages but brought with us especially. As India sank below the horizon before our eyes we tossed the topees into the tumbling white wake of water behind the ship. This was goodbye to a land we loved, and done in the traditional manner of the old days.

Geoffrey and Joan garlanded on leaving Shillong, 1970

153